THE WRIGHT BROTHERS

FIRST IN FLIGHT

MILESTONES
IN
AMERICAN HISTORY

THE TREATY OF PARIS

THE MONROE DOCTRINE

THE TRANSCONTINENTAL RAILROAD

THE ELECTRIC LIGHT

THE WRIGHT BROTHERS

THE STOCK MARKET CRASH OF 1929

SPUTNIK/EXPLORER I

THE CIVIL RIGHTS ACT OF 1964

THE WRIGHT BROTHERS

FIRST IN FLIGHT

SAMUEL WILLARD CROMPTON

CHELSEA HOUSE
PUBLISHERS
An imprint of Infobase Publishing

YA
629.13
CRO

Cover: Orville Wright soars over the water shortly after takeoff during one of the Wright Brothers' last glider flights.

The Wright Brothers: First in Flight

Copyright © 2007 by Infobase Publishing

Chelsea House
An imprint of Infobase Publishing
132 West 31st Street
New York, NY 10001

ISBN 10: 0-7910-9356-5
ISBN 13: 978-0-7910-9356-6

Library of Congress Cataloging-in-Publication Data
Crompton, Samuel Willard.
  The Wright brothers : first in flight / Samuel Willard Crompton.
     p. cm. — (Milestones in American history)
  Includes bibliographical references and index.
  ISBN 0-7910-9356-5 (hardcover)
  1. Wright, Orville, 1871-1948—Juvenile literature. 2. Wright, Wilbur, 1867–1912—Juvenile literature. 3. Aeronautics—United States—Biography—Juvenile literature. 4. Inventors—United States—Biography—Juvenile literature. 5. Aeronautics—United States—History—Juvenile literature. I. Title. II. Series.
  TL540.W7C75 2007
  629.130092'273—dc22   2006034131

Series design by Erik Lindstrom
Cover design by Ben Peterson

Printed in the United States of America

Bang NMSG 10 9 8 7 6 5 4 3 2 1

This book is printed on acid-free paper.

CONTENTS

A Perfect Circle

Today we call them the Wright brothers, but to friends they were Will and Orv. They were like most brothers, alike in some respects, very different in others. But by the summer of 1904, they were working together and doing great things in the air.

For the previous three summers, they had experimented at Kitty Hawk, on the Outer Banks of North Carolina. But in 1904, they were working closer to home, at a place called Huffman Prairie, about eight miles outside their hometown of Dayton, Ohio.

Will and Orv had made great progress during their time at Kitty Hawk, but certain accomplishments had eluded them. One was flying in a circle. Birds do it with seemingly great ease, and it was frustrating to the brothers to fly in a straight line all the time; actually, there were days when they were lucky to do

After becoming the first individuals to make a powered, sustained, and controlled airplane flight in December 1903, the Wright brothers set out to improve their flyer. Pictured here is their aircraft Flyer II, which they built in 1904 and tested at Huffman Prairie, outside Dayton, Ohio.

that. Flying certainly was not easy. In a major speech given to a Chicago society, Will said there were two ways to learn the secrets of flight. One was to sit on a fence and watch the birds, which gave a good deal of instruction; and the other was to fly kites and eventually get in the air oneself. Practice, in other words, was the key.

The Wright brothers practiced all that summer. They practiced on Huffman Prairie, which was very different from the sands of Kitty Hawk. On the positive side, the green grass provided an easier "drop" or "fall." On the negative side, the air blew around in a different way. Huffman Prairie is about 800 feet above sea level, and there is a lot of humidity. This combination meant that the air did not provide much lift and the Wright brothers had to acclimate to these conditions.

In May, they invited a group of local reporters to watch a flight. The reporters came on a particularly bad day for Will and Orv, because they failed to get off the ground. The reporters dismissed the Wright brothers as hopeless and went to cover better news stories. This seemed like bad luck for the brothers at the time, but it turned out for the better. Left alone, without the pressure of prying eyes, the Wrights were able to get more work done. The only drawback was that there was no one to witness or record what they accomplished. However, fate stepped in, and sent Amos I. Root.

THE WITNESS

In 1904, Root was 64 years old. Born and bred in Medina, Ohio, he was a self-made man who had become fascinated with bees in his youth. By his 30s, he had devised a hive from which one could extract honey while keeping the bees alive; this became the basis of the A.I. Root Company, which still exists today. Also, while he was in his 30s, Root had established a trade magazine called *Gleanings in Bee Culture.* He was the editor and chief editorial writer for many years, but he had given it up about 10 years before meeting the Wright brothers, leaving the business in the hands of his capable sons. Suddenly with more free time than in the past, Root became fascinated with things like bicycles and automobiles. He often claimed to have had the first European-style bicycle in Ohio and one of the first automobiles in the state. Root was a deeply religious man, but one who thought religion and science could work together. Learning of the Wright brothers, he revved up his automobile and made a 200-mile trip to see them in September 1904.

THE FIRST CIRCLE

The Wrights were suspicious of most outsiders, but they accepted Root. The white-haired man may have reminded them of their own father, Bishop Milton Wright, who was seldom around to see their flights, but had constantly encouraged them. Like Root, Bishop Wright did not see a conflict between religious faith and scientific investigation. The Wright brothers had grown up with all sorts of periodicals and magazines around the house, writings that opened their eyes to numerous subjects. Root became a welcome presence, and he was there on September 20 to serve as one of the first true eyewitnesses of manned flight. (There had been quite a few observers at Kitty Hawk, but none had much writing talent.)

The Wrights were enthusiastic photographers, but they were too occupied to capture the events of September 20; therefore, it is fortunate that Wilbur recorded the events of the day in his logbook. His first entry for the morning flight was as follows: "W. W. Cloudy. And. N.W. Wind [EN] a.m. distance 315 multiplied by a equals 2520 feet."[1] From this short and simple entry, we learn that the first flight on September 20 was by Wilbur Wright, and that he covered 2,520 feet. The second entry runs as follows: "Rain. N.E. wind [in]p.m. Completed circle. Distance 510 multiplied by 8 = 4080 [feet]."[2] The key words here are "completed circle." Nine months had passed since the Wright brothers had first flown at Kitty Hawk, North Carolina, but they had never been able to fly in a complete, 360-degree circle until that day. At the very bottom of the notebook page is the simple entry "Root present." In other words, the Wright brothers had a witness to their accomplishment.

Wilbur and Orville asked Amos Root not to publish the results of what he had seen until they informed their competitors. They gave their permission two months later, and readers of *Gleanings in Bee Culture* received the news when they opened their first issue of the new year, 1905.

THE ESSAY

Root's article began in dramatic fashion: "Dear friends, I have a wonderful story to tell you—a story that, in some respects, out rivals the Arabian Night's fables—a story, too, with a moral that I think many of the younger ones need, and perhaps some of the older ones too, if they will heed it."[3] Root then praised the Wright brothers and made a special example of them, suggesting that they stood out from ordinary people:

Although Wilbur and Orville Wright may have gained an interest in aviation when their father brought home a mechanical flying toy in the late 1870s, their interest did not become apparent until they read an article about German glider Otto Lilienthal in *McClure's* in 1894. Wilbur (left) and Orville are pictured here in 1903; less than a year before their first successful flight.

These two, perhaps by accident, or maybe as a matter of taste, began studying the flights of birds and insects. From this they turned their attention to what has been done in the way of enabling man to fly. They not only studied nature, but they procured the best books, and I think I may say all the papers, the world contains on the subject. When I first became acquainted with them, and expressed a wish to read up all there was on the subject, they showed me a library that astonished me; and I soon found they were far early first, not only in regard to our present knowledge, but everything that had been done in the past.

These boys (they are men now), instead of spending their summer vacation with crowds, and with such crowds as are often questionable, as so many do, went away by themselves to a desert place by the sea coast [Kitty Hawk, North Carolina].

You and I have in years past found enjoyment and health in sliding downhill on the snow; but these boys went off to that sandy waste on the Atlantic coast to slide downhill too; but instead of sliding on snow and ice they slid *on air*. With a gliding machine made of sticks and cloth they learn to glide and sore [sic] from the top of the hill to the bottom; and by making not only hundreds but *more than a thousand* experiments, they became so proficient in guiding these gliding machines that they could sail like a bird and control its movements up and down as well as sideways.[4]

Was Root exaggerating about the amount of time the Wrights put into their experiments? Perhaps; however, he went on to describe their experiments in 1904 at Huffman Prairie:

At first there was considerable trouble about getting the machine up in the air and the engine well up to speed. They did this by running along a single rail track perhaps 200 feet long. It was also, in the early experiments, found advisable to run against the wind, because they could then have a greater time to practice in the air and not get so far away from the building where it was stored. Since they can come around to the starting point, however, they can start with the wind even *behind* them; and with a strong wind behind it is an easy matter to make even *more* than a mile a minute.[5]

A mile a minute might sound unimpressive today, but one must remember that Amos Root was writing in a time when the greatest speed achieved by most people was either on a bicycle, or in a railroad car. Root then described the actual moment of flight:

The operator takes his place lying flat on his face. This position offers less resistance to the wind. The engine is started and got up to speed. The machine is held until ready to start by a sort of trap to be sprung when all is ready; then with a tremendous flapping and snapping of the four-cylinder engine, the huge machine springs aloft. When it first turned that circle, and came near the starting point, I was right in front of it; and I said then, and I believe still, it was one of the grandest sites, if not the grandest sight, of my life. Imagine a locomotive that has left its track, and is climbing up in the air right toward you—a locomotive without any wheels, we will say, but with white wings instead we will further say—a locomotive made of aluminum. Well, now, imagine this white locomotive, with wings that spread 20 feet each way, coming right toward you with a tremendous flap of its propellers, and you will have something like what I saw.[6]

Several people had witnessed the flight at Kitty Hawk on December 17, 1903. A few people had traveled to Huffman Prairie at different times during the summer of 1904 and witnessed different flights. But Root just happened to come at the time when the Wright brothers were about to execute one of their most difficult maneuvers, the first perfect circle in the air, and he was privileged to witness it. Thanks to the photograph that shows the two brothers, Wilbur Wright's logbook, and Amos Root's magazine essay, we can reconstruct and even, to some extent, reexperience the dramatic events of September 20, 1904.

Midwestern Boys

The Wright brothers were, like most people, products of their environment. They grew up with a particular way of looking at the world, one shaped primarily by their father.

THE WRIGHTS' PARENTS

Born in 1828, Milton Wright grew up in Indiana and Ohio at a time when the region was increasingly a battleground between those who supported abolition and those pushing for slavery. There were no slaves, officially, in Indiana and Ohio, but there were plenty of people who sympathized with slaveholders, and the area experienced its share of strife.

The young Milton Wright became a passionate abolitionist. By the time he was raising a family of his own, the slave issue had been settled, once and for all, by the Civil War. But still, Milton Wright carried the memories of that conflict with him, and, when he became a leading churchman, he brought what one might call an "us versus them" attitude to his work: There must be no compromise with the enemy, whether a pro-slavery agitator, or, in the case of his church, an enemy like the Masonic secret society.

There was a powerful anti-Masonic group in the Midwest; there had even been a political party with that title. As he rose in the Church of the United Brethren in Christ, Milton Wright became an outspoken opponent of secret societies. He told all his parishioners never to join one, and, when he became a bishop of the church, he used his prominent role to carry on the fight.

It was not a pleasant, or even a successful fight. Bishop Wright was a man of uncompromising character, and even charisma, but he had a stubborn streak of self-righteousness that worked against him. Many times his outspokenness got him into trouble, and there were occasions when other church leaders tried to force him to resign. He always fought back, and, as the years passed, he came to rely on his sons, Will in particular, to be advocates for his cause. They never let him down.

In 1859, Milton Wright (not yet a bishop) married Susan Catherine Koerner, who had been one of his students at Hartsville College. She was the daughter of a German wagon-wheel maker who had immigrated to the United States in 1818. She seems to have shared her husband's "us versus them" way of looking at the world, but she was also devoted to her domestic duties. Susan Wright was bright in most ways, but most of all she was mechanically inclined. Her sons later attributed much of their aptitude with mechanical devices to her.

THE WRIGHT CHILDREN

Milton and Susan Wright had five children. Reuchlin, the eldest, was born in 1861, and Lorin followed a year later. There was a gap of six years between Reuchlin and Wilbur, who was born in 1867. Then there was another four-year gap between Wilbur and Orville, who was born in 1871. The youngest was a daughter, Katharine, born in 1874. In total, the five siblings spanned a gap of 13 years—not huge, but enough to create two separate groups in the family, and one outsider.

Wilbur was the most self-possessed member of a rather self-possessed family. From Bishop Wright and his wife, the children inherited a powerful streak of what would today be called "know-it-all-ness." Each family member was determined to contribute something special or unusual to society. All tried in their unique way, but Wilbur might thank his circumstances for his success.

Certainly, he never complained about being the middle child; complaining was just not part of the Wright way. But, from an early age, Wilbur was sandwiched decisively in the middle, with two brothers who were five and six years older, and one brother and one sister who were four and seven years younger. There was no way to bridge this gap. Wilbur was alone as the middle child of the family.

His older siblings, Reuchlin and Lorin, both grew up rather quickly. By their mid-20s, they had both gone to college and married, with Reuchlin settling in Kansas and Lorin settling in Dayton, Ohio, just a few blocks from the family homestead. Lorin soon had three children who became regular visitors at the Wright home. Wilbur was a devoted uncle, but Orville was better at the task, which he did not see as work at all.

AN ABRUPT CHANGE

A physical accident provided the change that later led the brothers on the path to invention. By age 18, Wilbur was an excellent student. His parents hoped he would go to Yale and eventually to divinity school so he might follow in his father's footsteps. There is no proof that Wilbur was opposed to becoming a minister; rather, of all the five Wright children, Wilbur was the closest to his father, both in temperament and outlook. But sometime that year he suffered a physical injury that changed all these hopes and plans.

While he was ice skating, someone's ice hockey stick hit Wilbur square in the mouth and chin. Several teeth were knocked out,

In 1871, the Wrights moved to Dayton, Ohio, where they settled into this house at 7 Hawthorn Street. Despite being forced to move quite frequently because their father was a bishop in the Church of the United Brethren in Christ, the Wright family owned the home until 1914.

and he became permanently self-conscious about it, leading to the closed-mouth expression shown in most photographs of him. Even worse, Wilbur developed a slight heart condition just days later, brought on by the impact and the intense shock. College was ruled out—at least temporarily.

Wilbur did not leave the family home while he was in his early 20s; in fact, one might say he never left at all, because he remained a dutiful son to his parents, and a kind of surrogate parent to his younger siblings, for the rest of his life. Stricken by the accident and injury, Wilbur stayed home and became the caretaker for his mother, who had fallen ill with tuberculosis.

He spent about three years taking care of her. He carried her downstairs in the morning, fed and washed her, and carried her upstairs in the evening.

Why had all this fallen to Wilbur and not his father? The truth is that, although he was an admirable man in many respects, Bishop Wright appears to have been absent where home matters were concerned. He was much happier tending to his duties as bishop than he was caring for his invalid wife. No harsh words appear to have passed between father and son; it was almost as if they implicitly understood that Bishop Wright was concerned with the "outside" world and that he left the difficult "inside" tasks to his third child.

By the time Susan Koerner Wright died in 1889, Wilbur had become a singular kind of man, one truly versed in home care, but lacking a venue for his intellectual talents. At about this time, he and his younger brother, Orville, became much closer. Within a few years, they would form such a close partnership that the world still refers to them as the Wright brothers.

They started with printing. Orville built a printing press in the late 1880s. During this time, a printing expert from Chicago happened to stop by. Looking at the press, he declared that it certainly did work, though he was not sure how. Orville and Wilbur worked together, developing stories for what they called the *West Side News* and then the *Evening Item*. They also printed the *Dayton Tattler*, a weekly newspaper for Dayton's African-American community. Through this endeavor, they made the acquaintance of Paul Laurence Dunbar, who would go on to become one of the first major twentieth-century black poets. Later, Dunbar wrote a tribute to Orville:

> Orville Wright is out of sight
> In the printing business
> No other mind is half as bright
> As his'n is.[7]

The Wrights enjoyed the printing business, but by the early 1890s, they were ready to try something else—bicycles.

BICYCLES

The first bicycles were introduced to the United States sometime in the 1870s, but the first models were not very popular. They had enormous front wheels and tiny back wheels, creating a serious imbalance. These old-style bicycles are visually appealing, but they could never sustain any sort of speed; they were much more for show than sport. Then came the "safety" bicycle of the 1880s and 1890s.

The *safety* part meant that the two tires were of equal size, allowing the rider to achieve and maintain balance. The first safety bicycles appeared at about the time Susan Wright died, and her two youngest sons became interested in the new fad. Wilbur bought a bicycle for $80 and Orville bought another for $160. That was a lot of money in those days, considering that this was a time when a common laborer sometimes made as little as $500 per year. The brothers both took to bicycling, but Orville was more involved in the activity: He entered races and reveled in the prestige it brought him.

Orville had been very much the kid brother to this point, but he was actually better developed socially. He and their younger sister, Katharine, formed a close bond early on, and Orville—though not as brilliant as Wilbur—had a variety of interests. He played the guitar; he sang a bit; and he had tinkered with a printing press by the time he was 18. Now he was ready to join his older brother in a serious endeavor. And so, they formed a partnership and established the Wright Cycle Company.

Bicyles were indeed the rage in the 1890s. Millions of Americans bought them and took to the roads. The automobile was still in its infancy, and the bicycle appeared to be the sole means of freedom and liberation. Americans of all ages and classes took to the new toy. The Wright brothers started by repairing other people's bicycles, but they soon began to design two or three of their own lines of bicycles, including one that they named for a Revolutionary War ancestor on their father's side of the family.

THE NOTION OF FLIGHT

No one knows for sure exactly when the Wright brothers became fascinated by flight. It is true that their father had brought home a mechanical flying toy when they were very young (they called it a "bat"), but there is no indication in their letters or actions that flight was important to them until the mid-1890s, when they became aware of the German glider Otto Lilienthal.

McClure's magazine was only a couple of years old when it published an astonishing series of photos and text on "The Flying Man" in the summer of 1894. Lilienthal, then 46 years old, was profiled as an enthusiastic experimenter, having designed a new type of glider that imitated the actions of birds. Lilienthal's glider looked much like a bird that had spread its wings. He sat or stood in the middle, twisting his arms or legs to control the craft. He could not "take off" from level ground; instead, he had to run or be pushed down a hill into the breeze. But even with the simplicity of the machine, the results, shown in photographs, were remarkable. Up until then, people had only traveled through the air in balloons, which, being much weightier and bulkier, did not allow the pilot to experience the true sensation of flight. Lilienthal described the hardships in his work:

> There are still prominent investigators who will not see that the arched or vaulted wing includes the secret of the art of flight. As we came upon the track of this idea, my brother and I, who were then young and wholly without means, used to spare from our breakfasts, penny by penny, the money to

During his life, German aviator Otto Lilienthal made more than 2,000 flights in his mono and biplane gliders. Lilienthal, who is pictured here in the mid-1890s during a flight, inspired the Wright brothers to pursue careers in aviation.

prosecute our investigations; and often the "struggle for life" compelled us to interrupt them indefinitely.[8]

No further mention was made of Lilienthal's brother, but the inventor himself went on to design his gliders and to log as many as 500 hours of flight. He described, in *McClure's*, the sensational experience: "No one can realize how *substantial* the air is, until he feels its supporting power beneath him. It inspires confidence at once. With flat wings it would be almost impossible to guard against a fall. With arched wings it is possible to

THE MONTGOLFIERS

Aviator Brothers

It is interesting to see that Otto Lilienthal and his brother had worked closely together, as the Wright brothers would do. But there was another pair of brothers who had made history in balloon flight.

At the time of the Revolutionary War, many French inventors were inspired by the presence in Paris of the American inventor and diplomat Benjamin Franklin. It was a time when all things seemed possible, and Parisians were thrilled at the news that two Frenchmen had invented a balloon that would soar over their fair city.

Born and raised in east-central France, the Montgolfier brothers were members of a very large family that earned its fortune in papermaking. One of the elder brothers, Joseph, was considered something of a spendthrift, while the youngest brother, Etienne, was believed to be the one who would take over the family company. Strangely, these two oddly matched brothers pioneered the development of a hot-air balloon, which they launched in June 1783.

King Louis XVI and Queen Marie Antoinette were intrigued, and the Montgolfier brothers were quickly summoned to Paris, where, in September 1783, they sent up their balloon over the city. The brothers had promised their father that they would not pilot the balloon, so they sent up a pig, a fowl, and a sheep. All three animals survived the flight, which was witnessed by the king, queen, and, from his hotel window, Benjamin Franklin.

The brothers kept their word to their father; they never flew themselves. The first man to pilot a balloon took off in October of that year, and a couple of years later another Frenchman became the first person to cross the English Channel. Ballooning quickly became a sensation in the 1780s and 1790s, but, by the early 1800s, it was no longer popular. It did not become important again until the U.S. Civil War when the Union Army used balloons for gathering information.

sail against a moderate breeze at an angle of not more than six degrees to the horizon."[9]

Meanwhile, in 1896, Orville Wright had become sick. His brother Wilbur was nursing him back to health after an attack of typhoid when the brothers learned Lilienthal had died after falling from his glider. He had survived long enough to say, "Sacrifices must be made." This would become a motto for experimenters of all kinds. Up until this time, the Wright brothers had not conducted a single experiment of their own, but perhaps the idea was growing in their minds. Two more years passed before they began to experiment.

In the spring of 1899, Wilbur Wright penned a letter to the director of the Smithsonian Institution in Washington, D.C. detailing his interest in flight:

> I have been interested in the problem of mechanical and human flight ever since as a boy I constructed a number of bats of various sizes after the style of Cayley's and Penaud's machines. My observations since have only convinced me more firmly that human flight is possible and practicable. It is only a question of knowledge and skill just as in all acrobatic feats. Birds are the most perfectly trained gymnasts in the world and are specially well fitted for this work, and it may be that man will never equal them, but no one who has watched a bird chasing an insect or another bird can doubt that feats are performed which require three or four times the effort required in ordinary flight. I believe that simple flight at least is possible to man and that the experiments and investigations of a large number of independent workers will result in the accumulation of information and knowledge and skill which will finally lead to accomplished flight.[10]

This letter was the beginning of a road that would lead upward, outward, and eventually carry Wilbur and Orville Wright to the heights of fame and fortune.

The
Competition

When Wilbur Wright wrote to the Smithsonian, he did not know that its director was himself driven by the idea of human flight. So, too, were a small but growing number of other men throughout the world. Just as the automobile had been invented in several places at almost the same time, many individuals were also looking into the possibilities of flight at the turn of the twentieth century. Two of these people were Alexander Graham Bell and Samuel Pierpont Langley.

The former was one of the most famous men of the time, perhaps even of the century. Born in Edinburgh, Scotland, in 1847, Bell had moved to Canada as a young man, and then to the United States, settling first in Boston and then in Washington, D.C. In 1876, he had invented and patented the telephone, but throughout his life, he primarily thought of himself as an educator of the deaf. By 1899, the year Wilbur Wright wrote to the

Smithsonian, Bell had become a prominent figure and was close friends with Samuel Langley, the director of the Smithsonian.

Born in Roxbury, Massachusetts, in 1834, Langley had taken a roundabout way to achieving success. He had worked as a draftsman and engineer in his youth, and, without ever going to college, he had become head of an astronomical observatory in Pittsburgh, Pennsylvania. Interested in understanding the impact of solar radiation, Langley had conducted many experiments over the years. His methods were always based on science, which is illustrated by his painstaking drawings of sunspots. By the 1890s, Langley had become fascinated with the possibilities of flight, and he brought his good friend Alexander Bell into the fold.

Each of the two men were much older than Wilbur Wright and both of them had had ample time to observe nature—that is to say, birds—in action. But, unlike Wilbur Wright, Langley and Bell were convinced that a powerful engine, or motor, was the key to success in flight. Wilbur Wright had not yet come up with his own philosophy, but it would develop very rapidly over the next few years. It was based on observing birds, imitating their movements, and learning how to balance a craft in the air. Wilbur thought that these issues should be addressed first, before any attempt at using motors.

Langley and Bell were no slouches when it came to observation, but they did not consider balance that important. What mattered was that the craft should move through the air; the more rapidly it did so, the more likely it would stay airborne. There was science behind their thinking, but they also hoped to avoid the kind of trial and error for which Wilbur and Orville Wright would become famous.

Soon after he became director of the Smithsonian in 1887, Langley turned his attention to motorized flight. He had a mechanical arm built in a workroom of the Smithsonian and soon decided that the way to launch a flying craft was to fling it into the air and then have the motor take over. The safest way to fling such a craft was to do so over water, so Langley had a

American astronomer and aeronautical pioneer Samuel Pierpont Langley competed against the Wright brothers to construct the first aircraft capable of human flight. Unfortunately for Langley, his aircraft, which is depicted in this painting, made two unsuccessful flights in 1903, and the Wright brothers achieved sustained flight first.

houseboat anchored on the Potomac River, from which occasional experiments were made. He achieved his greatest success in the summer of 1896, when his Aerodrome Number 1 was launched into the air and remained airborne for a few seconds.

Wilbur Wright may have known about the 1896 test, but he did not know that the U.S. government had recently allocated $50,000 for experiments with motorized flight. Langley had discretion over the first $25,000, and he would need to demonstrate some results to obtain the second half. He was helped along by his friendship with Bell—who was admired by the entire Washington, D.C., community—and by the start of the Spanish–American War, which persuaded President William

McKinley that some type of flying craft (the word airplane was not yet coined) would be useful for surveillance.

Wilbur Wright was clearly not much of a concern to people like Samuel Langley and Alexander Bell. In fact, Langley had not received the letter Wilbur sent because he was away on holiday. A lower official at the Smithsonian Institution promptly sent back a number of pamphlets and periodicals, all of which may have helped Wilbur to some degree.

A MENTAL BREAKTHROUGH

Years later, Wilbur Wright would claim that he "saw" better with his imagination than with his eyes. This is actually true of many people at certain times; it is sometimes possible to visualize something that does not yet exist. But Wilbur had this ability to an uncommon degree, and he had the gritty type of resourcefulness to follow through when he was inspired. And that is what happened in the early summer of 1899.

Just weeks after he received materials from the Smithsonian, Wilbur was working alone in the bicycle shop. He had in his hands an empty cardboard box that had previously held a bicycle inner tube. Wilbur absentmindedly twisted the ends of the rectangular box while he began to think. Then, with his "mind's eye," he looked down and saw that the two ends were twisting, or warping, in a manner not unlike what birds do with their wings. (A little later, this process would be called "wing warping".)

As he looked down, Wilbur believed he had uncovered one of the great mysteries of bird flight. Many observers had concluded that a bird tucked one wing close to its body to make a turn, but Wilbur's observations of birds—especially buzzards—had dismissed that idea. In the ends of the cardboard box, he saw what birds did: They twisted, or warped, their wings in order to raise one wing and lower the other. The result was that they could maintain their balance.

It was an astonishing breakthrough. One wonders why it had not been discovered before, either by Wilbur Wright or someone else. The answer is that birds move too quickly for humans to catch these movements with the naked eye. Once one knows that birds warp their wings, it makes perfect sense, and a person may feel that he or she actually sees it in action, but very few people have eyesight that sharp. About a dozen years earlier, the advent of modern photography made observation of birds in flight easier. Wilbur had been able to examine several books with photographs of birds; but it still remains unlikely that anyone would have made this breakthrough with the physical eye alone: Action of the "mind's eye," or the imagination, was required.

THE FIRST KITES

There was nothing new about kites during the Wright brothers' time; they had been around for some time. But Wilbur started to experiment with his notion of wing warping, and it was at about this time that Orville became his partner in the process.

It has long been a matter of controversy as to whether the brothers were equal partners in their endeavors. In early letters and applications, Wilbur Wright referred to "my idea," "my project," and so forth, but by the latter part of 1900, he consistently used the term *we*. Early biographers of the Wright brothers thought of them as a team and perhaps they became so over the years. But in the early years, it was clearly Wilbur who supplied the larger drive and imagination. This is not to belittle Orville's contributions, which were important, but rather to suggest that the older brother was the "leader" of the twosome.

By the spring of 1900, Wilbur and Orville had built several kites and experimented in fields near Dayton, Ohio. They used strings and pulleys to create a wing-warping effect and found that it worked. But they needed more room and stronger breezes to make more successful tests, and they also needed some advice

By 1900, the Wright brothers had built several model gliders that they used to simulate air flight. These "kites" were controlled through the use of strings and pulleys, which the Wright brothers used to create a wing-warping effect.

from an aviation expert. So, around Memorial Day of 1900, Wilbur wrote to Chicago engineer and aviator Octave Chanute.

The letter began: "For some years I have been afflicted with the belief that flight is possible to man. My disease has increased in severity and I feel that it will soon cost me an increased amount of money if not my life. I have been trying to arrange my affairs in such a way that I can devote my entire time for a few months to experiment in this field."[11]

During this time, Wilbur and Orville still ran the bicycle shop. They did all right financially, but they were especially busy during the spring and summer months, when their neighbors wanted to be out on the road. The letter continued: "The flight of the buzzard and similar sailers is a convincing

OCTAVE CHANUTE
(1832–1910)

A Pioneer in Aviation

Octave Chanute was born in France and came to the United States with his family at an early age. He grew up in the Midwest and went to school in New Orleans. By 1900, the year in which he first heard from Wilbur Wright, Chanute had become something of a legend in aviation and engineering. He helped design a great bridge over the Mississippi River and was a founder of the Chicago School of Engineering. He was successful to the point where he could take extended vacations to places as far away as Egypt. Yet he still had one great ambition: to see men fly in the air.

During the late 1890s, Chanute brought together a small group of aviators who flew gliders that he had built. They took off from the sandy beaches of Lake Michigan and made some progress, but none of the gliders incorporated the notion of wing warping (which Wilbur Wright had just discovered). Chanute was too old to partake in these experiments himself, but he nudged, cajoled, and flattered his gliders until they were willing to take risks. He was very comfortable financially and had no need for more money, but he did want to play a role in the development of flight.

When he first heard from the Wright brothers in 1900, Chanute was impressed because they clearly knew a good deal about the subject. During the next five years, he was their biggest backer, but they came to realize that he was most interested in seeing someone attain human flight, rather than caring solely about them. Relations between Chanute and the Wrights soured over the years, resulting in some explosive and bitter letters in 1910. There was an effort to repair the damage, but Chanute died later that year.

Chanute was unusual among aviators—and aviator backers—in that he was willing to look at all aspects of a problem instead of concentrating on one. He knew what Langley and Bell were doing, and he knew about the Wrights. Perhaps he could have cultivated the relationship between the two groups, but that might also have hindered the competition that led to the first flight in December 1903.

demonstration of the value of skill, and the partial needlessness of motors. It is possible to fly without motors, but not without knowledge & skill."[12]

It seems that this young man, with no college degree or professional training, thought he could avoid the path being taken by the director of the Smithsonian. He intended to practice balance in the air, without the aid of motors. He went on to write in the letter: "My observation of the flight of buzzards leads me to believe that they regain their lateral balance, when partly overturned by a gust of wind, by a torsion of the tips of the wings. If the rear edge of the right wing tip is twisted upward and the left downward the bird becomes an animated windmill and instantly begins to turn, a line from its head to its tail being the axis."[13]

Wilbur concluded the letter by asking Chanute's help in finding a suitable location to do some experimentation. Perhaps he thought the older man would suggest some nearby, easily found place, but Chanute wrote back, speaking of the favorable winds in San Diego, California; St. James City, Florida; and "perhaps even better locations can be found on the Atlantic coasts of South Carolina or Georgia."[14] Whether he intended it or not, Chanute had directed the brothers in the direction of the place that is now synonymous with the Wright name: Kitty Hawk.

Kitty Hawk
I and II

Kitty Hawk stands on the narrow shifting sand that defines the Outer Banks of North Carolina. It was, and is, no easy place to live. Hurricanes sometimes affect the region, and warm waters from the south collide with colder ones, creating a very unstable climate. At least 600 ships have sunk off the Outer Banks of North Carolina, leading sailors to call it the "graveyard of the North Atlantic."

Kitty Hawk was even more remote and less accessible when the Wright brothers arrived there in 1900. Born and raised in the Midwest, they had never seen the ocean before. If not for the reading they had done, the brothers would have been poorly equipped to encounter the outside world. But thanks to their family library, they were familiar with far-off locations in Europe and Asia. (People would later observe that during

Wilbur's first visit to France, he knew more about the country than many French people.)

Wilbur set off for Kitty Hawk at the end of August 1900. The plan was for Wilbur to get to Kitty Hawk first, while Orville tended the bicycle shop. Orville would then join Wilbur, while their sister, Katharine, and a hired employee ran the shop in the brothers' absence. Bishop Wright was usually out of town, and he only found out about his sons' trip to North Carolina by a letter from Katharine, who said it would be a good vacation for the "boys" (they were 33 and 29), even if it didn't turn into anything greater.

Wilbur got off the train in Elizabethtown, North Carolina, in the midst of a massive heat wave. Being the sons of a bishop, the Wrights always dressed conservatively in long pants and shirts, as well as hats. Wilbur nearly fainted in the heat, but he managed to buy some spruce boards in town before boarding a boat for Kitty Hawk. Even though he was close to his destination, he found there were many people who never even heard of Kitty Hawk.

Thirty-six hours later, Wilbur arrived at sand-blown Kitty Hawk. It had about 60 full-time residents and a U.S. lifesaving station nearby that employed about seven more. Virtually all the people of Kitty Hawk were deeply tanned, having spent many years in the sun. Many of them were descendants of sailors who had come ashore after they had been shipwrecked off the coast.

As soon as he arrived in Kitty Hawk, Wilbur went straight to the home of Bill Tate, who had written a glowing testimonial to Wilbur describing Kitty Hawk's wonderful attributes. Bill Tate was the most "modern" resident of this distinctly old-fashioned place. His wife, Addie, was the postmistress, and they had two daughters.

Tate had advised Wilbur, by letter, that Kitty Hawk was an excellent place to conduct wind experiments because of the continually shifting breeze. But he had also warned that after mid-October, the weather got a "little rough" (an understatement if ever there was one). Wilbur knew that time was short, and soon after he arrived, he was stitching together the glider he hoped to fly.

Orville came about 10 days later. Soon everyone in the community addressed both of the brothers as "Mr. Wright." Orville described the conditions they faced:

> We have been having a fine time, altogether we have had the machine out three different days, from 2 to 4 hours each time. Monday night and all day Tuesday we had a terrific wind blowing 36 miles an hour. Wednesday morning the Kitty Hawkers were out early peering around the edge of the woods and out of their upstairs windows to see whether our camp was still in existence.[15]

Orville called it a "machine" but "kite" or "glider" would have been more accurate. The Wright brothers had built a thing of fragile beauty, which floated upward in a lovely way, but which could come crashing down at a moment's notice. One of the first people ever to get into it, and perhaps one of the first to "fly" anywhere, was young Tom Tate. About 10 years old, he was the nephew of Bill Tate, the man who had so warmly welcomed Wilbur a month earlier. Orville described Tom Tate in a letter to his sister, Katharine: "Tom is a small chap, about the size of Charles Millard, that can tell more big yarns than any kid of his size I ever saw. We took a picture of him as he came along the other day on his way home with a drum almost as large as he. The drum is a salt-water fish."[16]

Orville was the better storyteller of the brothers. He sent home letter after letter with amusing anecdotes, while Wilbur did most of his writing in the logbook. Both brothers were meticulous record keepers; if they made any breakthroughs in flight, they wanted to be able to recount the day, place, and time. Though experimenting with the glider, Wilbur continued to watch birds, of which there were thousands at Kitty Hawk: "The hen hawk can

Tom Tate, the nephew of Kitty Hawk resident Bill Tate, was the first person to fly one of the Wright brothers' gliders in North Carolina. Here, Tom poses with a drum fish in front of one of the Wrights' gliders in 1900.

rise faster than the buzzard and its motion is steadier. It displays less effort in maintaining its balance. Hawks are better soarers than buzzards but more often resort to flapping because they wish greater speed." Wilbur continued: "A damp day is unfavorable for soaring unless there is a high wind. No bird soars in a calm."[17] Both of the brothers, but Wilbur especially, based their thoughts on what they saw, rather than what they had learned or been taught in the past. Of course, very few people really *could* teach them anything about flight, because the art was so unknown.

All too soon, the flying season had come to an end. The Wright brothers left their glider at Kitty Hawk. Addie Tate promptly cut up the sateen parts to make dresses for her daughters. Back home in Dayton, Wilbur described what they had accomplished:

> We found no difficulty in establishing for-and-aft balance. The ease with which it was accomplished was a matter of great astonishment to us. It was so different from what the writings of other experimenters led us to expect. This may have been partly due to the steadiness of the wind, partly to the fixed position of the operator, and partly to a fortunate combination of circumstances of which we were not aware, but it is our hope that it was due to a new method. . . . We never found it necessary to shift the body.[18]

This was extraordinary. Otto Lilienthal and virtually all gliders who had come before him had moved their limbs to control the craft, to duck and maneuver with the wind. But the Wright brothers had found a more stable, and safer, means of accomplishing the same results by having the operator stay in one fixed place and by having him warp the wings through a series of string and wire lines. Yet, except for Octave Chanute, virtually no one who was involved with flying knew what the brothers had done at Kitty Hawk.

THE SECOND YEAR

By the spring of 1901, Wilbur and Orville were full partners in the enterprise; a matter that was not illustrated in their records or receipts, but in the letters of Wilbur, who now wrote of "our plan," "our intention," and so forth. What had been the brainchild of the older brother was now the passion of both.

The Wright brothers were far behind their competition in financing and development, but they had something their rivals did not: an exceptional ability to concentrate on a technical problem and to stick with it until it was solved. Their method of argument was once described by their mechanic,

Charlie Taylor, who said that the brothers' voices would rise and they would argue all the way around a problem, or idea, until Wilbur was ready to say that Orville was right, and Orville would say the same thing about Wilbur.

In 1901, they tried to improve on their achievements from the previous year. This time the brothers went together, and they arrived in Kitty Hawk in July rather than September. They had built a second glider, with full wing-warping ability, but they still had no motor. Both brothers believed that a motor was the last piece of the puzzle, which should be added when all matters of stability, steering, and balance had been solved.

By that time, the Wright brothers' project had become an obsession for the whole Wright family. Bishop Wright was as interested as anyone, and Katharine Wright had become the steady wheel who would manage the home—and, in a pinch, the bicycle shop—while the brothers were away. Lorin Wright, who lived in Dayton, was starting to become involved, too.

Wilbur and Orville moved the location for their second set of tests. Late in the 1900 flying season, they had noticed a series of outcroppings the locals called Kill Devil Hills: three prominent sand dunes, about a mile away from where they had experimented that year. When they went back in 1901, the brothers took their new glider to these hills and set about trying to beat the previous year's records.

They failed.

They tried, and failed again. Wilbur confided in his diary:

The most discouraging features of our experiments so far are these: The lift is not much over one third than indicated by the Lilienthal tables. As we had expected to devote a major portion of our time to experimenting in an 18-mile wind without much motion of the machine, we find that our hopes of obtaining actual practice in the air are decreased to about one fifth what we hoped.[19]

The Wright brothers' second glider, built in 1901, was an improvement from their first glider, but they were unable to achieve the same results as the year before. Here, Wilbur Wright lies in the prone position in his attempt to pilot their 1901 glider above the dunes of Kitty Hawk, North Carolina.

By this time, the brothers had identified three different forces that affect flight. *Lift* means the amount of pressure underneath the wings of the craft. *Drag* is the amount of downward pressure. The *angle of attack* (also called the angle of incidence) is the angle at which wind strikes a leading edge. The brothers already understood the mechanics of flight better than anyone of their time, yet they were unable to match their success from the year before. They knew their 1901 glider was better made than its predecessor; they also knew that their knowledge had expanded. What were they missing? Scientifically examining the matter, the Wright brothers slowly came to the conclusion that Lilienthal's mathematical tables were "off."

As they walked away from their second season of experiments, the brothers were more discouraged than at any previous time. It has never been entirely clear what Wilbur said to Orville on the trip home, but it was something to the effect that humans would not be able to fly for a very long time, perhaps not for the next hundred years.

CHANUTE TO THE RESCUE

At this critical stage, the Wright brothers were prepared to walk away from the entire project. They felt they had given it their best, and that perhaps they might have to give up their "hobby." But just a few days after they returned to Dayton, Wilbur received a letter from Octave Chanute asking him to give a speech to the Western Society of Engineers in Chicago.

Chanute did not understand, or agree with, all the brothers' calculations and theories, but he clearly had great respect for the two young men. The Western Society of Engineers was largely composed of self-made men like Chanute, who welcomed ingenuity and hard work. Fatigued from their experiments at Kitty Hawk, and discouraged from their lack of success, Wilbur was ready to turn Chanute down, but his younger sister, Katharine, intervened. This was no time to quit, she said. She and Orville prepared to make Wilbur, who did not care about style, look his very best, and he spruced up his ideas for the big talk, which he gave in late September 1901.

By now, Wilbur and Orville were concerned that other aviators might try to steal their ideas. But Wilbur revealed everything they had gone through, including many of the successes and failures they had so far encountered:

> The balancing of a gliding or flying machine is very simple in theory. It merely consists in causing the center of pressure

to coincide with the center of gravity. But in actual practice there seems to be an almost boundless incompatibility of temper which prevents their remaining peaceably together for a single instant, so that the operator, who in this case acts as peacemaker, often suffers injury to himself while attempting to bring them together.[20]

No one in attendance could have missed a central point. Wilbur spoke of the operator of the glider as a peacemaker between pressure and gravity, while the major work done by the Smithsonian, under Professor Langley's direction, had emphasized that the operator's main concern was the strength of the engine. The Wright brothers' approach was more modest in some ways, but also truly revolutionary. They used very complex mathematical tables to demonstrate how they had arrived at their opinions. Nearly everyone was impressed. Wilbur also described his and Orville's adventurous way of testing the air:

> If I take this piece of paper, and after placing it parallel with the ground, quickly let it fall, it will not settle down as a staid, sensible piece of paper ought to do, but it insists on contravening every recognized rule of decorum, turning over and darting hither and thither in the most erratic manner, much after the style of an untrained horse.[21]

True enough. But how did the Wright brothers attempt to train this horse?

> We only learn to appreciate it when we try to imitate it. Now, there are two ways of learning how to ride a fractious horse: one is to get on him and learn by actual practice how each motion and trick may be best met; the other is to sit on a fence and watch the beast a while, and then retire to the house and at leisure figure out the best way of overcoming his jumps and kicks.[22]

Octave Chanute, pictured here in 1908, was an engineer and aviation pioneer who frequently corresponded with the Wright brothers. In the 1890s, Chanute commissioned many gliders and helped generate interest in aviation through the publication of his book, *Progress in Flying Machines*.

There was no doubt about which method the Wrights favored. Chanute was pleased with the brothers and they with him. His invitation to Wilbur to speak in Chicago had motivated the brothers to return to the drawing board, but they would continue to work alone. They did not want anyone to steal the fruits of their labor.

Kitty Hawk
III

The winter of 1901 to 1902 was exceptionally busy for the Wrights. Having tasted disappointment, they now set their minds to developing their own mathematical tables. The experiments of 1901 had been a real letdown from those of 1900. The brothers could not believe that the glider of 1901 was inferior to the earlier one, because they designed, cut, and assembled it themselves. Therefore, within days of Wilbur's speech to the Chicago engineers, they decided the trouble must lie with the mathematical computations of earlier flight enthusiasts. Otto Lilienthal's tables were treated with great respect throughout the scientific community, but Wilbur and Orville decided to make their own.

Soon they set about making the world's first wind tunnel. Bicycles were still their livelihood, and the brothers put a circular test kit on top of the handlebars of one of their bikes. Riding around Dayton, Wilbur and Orville calculated the interference, the wind strength, and the amount of resistance offered to the circular motion tester. This was novel enough; one cannot imagine Langley or any of the other major inventors doing the same, but Wilbur and Orville then designed a more permanent wind tunnel, which was housed in their bicycle shop.

What they were trying to find was the value of an equation expressed as P tang a)/P90. This formula determines the lifting power of a curved surface at an angle to the wind. Sailors had known about the formula for centuries, but had never fully developed a means to test it. Wilbur reported the results to Chanute in October: "I am now absolutely certain that Lilienthal's table is very seriously in error, but that the error is not as great as I had previously estimated."[23] In November, Wilbur wrote a longer letter to Chanute, describing the errors in Lilienthal's thinking and computations. He described Lilienthal's calculations in detail:

> Lilienthal is very unfair to the plane. He greatly underestimates its lifting power, and exaggerates its drift, and thus falls into the absurdity of finding a tangential in a plane . . . However, his errors, on the whole, are so small compared with his truth, that his book must be considered an extraordinary one to be the work of a single man.[24]

By now, Wilbur and Orville Wright had passed the experts in the field. They knew more from day-to-day experimentation than Lilienthal had known, and they correctly estimated that he was far in advance of all the others. One can accuse the Wrights of being confident but never of being vain. They never offered any more information than they could back up with charts and tables; and perhaps it was fortunate for the history of science that the "experts" did not all know what the Wrights were doing. Their intuitive genius and attention to detail might have been continually debated in technical journals, which, from a modern point of view, would have been a tremendous waste of time.

When the Wrights headed to Kitty Hawk in the summer of 1902, they left home more confident than in the past. The bicycle shop was in the capable hands of Charlie Taylor; the household was in Katharine's charge; and their affairs were well enough in order for them to spend three months experimenting in North Carolina. The brothers found Kitty Hawk the same as always. The locals were as curious as ever, but no more convinced that the Wrights would ever achieve flight. There were no newspapers, no journalists, and very little else to distract the brothers from their work.

THE 1902 GLIDER

There had been two previous gliders, those of 1900 and 1901. The second was an improvement over the first in many respects, but the 1902 glider would stand out from the previous ones. For one, the brothers designed a fan, or tail, to accompany the craft. Until that point, the Wright gliders had included a front section, also called the elevator, but nothing in the rear. Through their wind-tunnel experiments, they realized that something in the rear was needed to both stabilize and help steer the craft. Obviously they wanted something very light, so they built a horizontal rudder that did not move.

The Wrights arrived in Kitty Hawk in August. They could not start experimenting right away, for they wanted to live in more comfort than before. A well was dug; the cabin was expanded; and a primitive type of airplane hangar was constructed. Due to all this work, the Wrights were not ready to begin experimenting until September.

By that time, they had established a system to get help from the locals. On days that were ideal for gliding, the brothers would fly a certain flag that brought some people over from Kitty Hawk or the U.S. lifesaving station. These people helped the Wrights carry the glider up a sandy dune and then ran along with it—practically carrying the glider—until the moment came to release the glider. At that point, everything depended on the wind.

UNDERSTANDING THE ELEMENTS OF FLIGHT

By 1902, the Wrights were on to many, though not all, of the aspects of flight. Other experimenters and theorists had come close, but none had been able to combine theory *and* experimentation.

The Wrights now understood "lift," meaning the amount of upward pressure exerted by the wind on the wings of a craft. They knew that their new glider had to accentuate lift and reduce the amount of drag. "Drag" means the downward push from the air above the wings. Essentially, anything that flies, whether a bird or a piece of folded paper, is precariously balanced between the forces of lift and drag. Too much of the former and the craft will move up too quickly, spinning out of control. Too much drag is even worse, for it will send the craft downward quickly, and usually expose it to side-swiping air currents that may flip it over.

There were other elements that affected flight, too, but it is important to concentrate here on the length and width of the wingspan and their ratio to the central part of the craft. By making their own mathematical equations, the Wrights were better able to shape their craft, settling on a 12-degree angle for the wings. Given that they were going to fly at Kitty Hawk—where the winds were different from elsewhere—they also edged the ends of the wings downward. This worked very well on sandy beaches, but it would create troubles at other locations.

All this begs the question: Could someone have worked these problems out without making dozens or hundreds of glides? A Leonardo da Vinci, perhaps; ordinary men and women had to experiment to test their theories.

When the Wrights returned to Kitty Hawk in 1902, they decided to expand their camp by constructing a hangar (pictured here) to house their glider. In addition, they dug a well and enlarged their cabin.

There were plenty of failures. Orville, in particular, seemed almost prone to near-death experiences. Time and again the craft would upend at the wrong moment, pitching him onto the sand. Wilbur took some falls, too, but most of the photographs from 1902 show Wilbur gliding, practically soaring about 40 feet above the ground. More than a century later, those photographs still captivate those who view them. There was something so supernaturally graceful about the glider, and Wilbur looked as if he had been destined from birth to fly. Perhaps he was.

Inevitably, there were troubles. The craft was wondrously made, but it took a beating from the numerous glides, descents, and landings, and it had to be repaired on a frequent basis. There was also the sheer matter of exhaustion; it was tiring to carry the flyer up those sandy slopes. Everyone seemed to wear out except the Wright brothers. One factor that may have sustained them through the fatigue was the knowledge that they would always have a break on Sunday; the brothers had promised their father, long ago, that they would always treat Sunday as a day of rest.

In addition to dealing with wear and tear, the new tail, or fin, also caused some trouble. Lying in the cradle, the operator now had to adjust, pull, or release three wires at once, one for his right wing, another for his left, and a third for the tail. The solution to this problem came from an aviation enthusiast and friend of the Wrights—Dr. George Spratt. One night, he and Orville sat up late talking, and they agreed to fix the wires so that the operator would only have to adjust the elevator and warping mechanism. The tail would be wired directly into the warping wire. In retrospect, these adjustments might seem simple. But the Wrights had no one—except for the occasional helper like George Spratt—to guide them. Yet they still were achieving more than anyone had before. Throughout their experimentation, the competition between themselves and Langley drove them. They rarely spoke of it, but Wilbur and Orville had a strong incentive to move as fast as possible. A big breakthrough came on Friday, October 10, 1902:

> The day opened with a calm, which was followed about 7 o'clock with a northeast wind that grew stronger & stronger as the day advanced. We took the machine to the Little Hill where we spent some time in practice, where Lorin [Wright] took pictures of Will gliding. In two of these glides he came to a stop high in the air, turned with one wing up, and landed with the wind blowing directly from the side of the machine.[25]

Wilbur made the day's longest glide, 280 feet. Even the observers could not have known how important this was. The Wrights had mastered balance and straight-ahead flight. All that their "machine" lacked now was a motor.

Unlike the Wright brothers, who financed their flight experiments, Samuel Pierpont Langley received funding from the U.S. government to develop an airplane. Although Langley's models achieved flight, he was not able to get a manned flight off the ground.

LANGLEY CONTACTS THE WRIGHTS

In the autumn of 1902, Samuel Langley had been experimenting for about six years. He had received a total of $50,000 from the U.S. government, but by 1902, the money had run out. Alexander Graham Bell had generously contributed, and Langley was using his own money, but he seemed as far from success as ever. His powerful motor, built in New York City, would not be ready for testing until the following year.

Now, in the autumn, Langley realized that the Wrights might achieve flight first. He had never met them, and had not seen any samples of their work, but he was in close com munication with Octave Chanute. Early in November, Langley sent a telegram to Kitty Hawk. In it, he asked them if he could come visit the brothers at their camp. Or, if not, could he have the pleasure of seeing them in Washington, D.C., during their trip home?

In a letter to Chanute, Wilbur described his answer: "We replied that it would scarcely be possible as we were intending to break camp in a few days. He made no mention of his experiments on the Potomac."[26] At this point, the Wright brothers were so close to achieving flight that they were not going to share their secrets.

The Magical
Moment

Orville did not exaggerate when he wrote to his sister, Katharine: "We now hold all the records! . . . The longest time in the air, the smallest angle of descent, and the highest wind!!!"[27]

All that they lacked was a motor. Returning to Dayton, the Wrights looked around to major manufacturers. They thought they could readily purchase a power motor to serve their needs, but they quickly found out otherwise. Motors were indeed being made throughout the United States, but none for this purpose. Most expert mechanics were concentrating on building automobile engines, far too large and heavy to mount on a glider. Eventually the Wrights decided they would have to find another source. Given time, the Wrights could probably have built a motor on their own, but they were short on time and they were much more skilled with wood than metal. Therefore

In 1903, Charlie Taylor designed the first four-cylinder engine for an aircraft. Amazingly, Taylor was able to construct his aluminum, water-cooled engine from scratch in just six weeks.

it made perfect sense to hire Charlie Taylor to build the world's first "flying engine."

Born on an Illinois farm in 1868, Taylor was one year younger than Wilbur and three years older than Orville. He was seemingly destined to be a farmer, but circumstances had pulled him away, and by 1902, he was a mechanic living in Dayton. The Wrights hired him in 1901 to run the bicycle shop in their absence, and they noticed he was a fine worker, both steady and reliable. So they turned to Taylor to build a motor for the 1903 Wright Flyer.

There were no special designs for the motor. Wilbur simply showed Taylor what he wanted, a strong motor small enough to be mounted on a plane. Taylor obtained a big piece of steel and began cutting, and within six weeks he had designed and built a motor. Even with all the other remarkable instances of ingenuity, Taylor's swift creation of a motor stands out as one of the most impressive.

But that was not all the Wrights had to worry about. Not only did they have to design the motor, they also had to design the propellers. Again, the Wrights had expected that someone had already solved this issue, only to find that the propellers that had been designed were inadequate for their flyer. The propeller of the day worked well enough in the water, where it moved a boat forward, but it was not designed for flight, where the propeller would also have to interact with the wind.

Once again, Wilbur took the lead. He designed and cut his own propellers from wood. For this intricate task he only had the use of a lathe in the bicycle shop, and, as always, the Wrights were short on time. They knew that Langley had planned a big demonstration sometime in 1903, and they were now faced with the possibility of competition from abroad.

BIGMOUTHED CHANUTE

From the very beginning, Octave Chanute had been something of a mixed bag. The brothers had been flattered when he first corresponded with them and had provided them with valuable information. But Chanute did not really seem to understand how revolutionary their work was. By the time he began writing to the Wrights, he was in his late 60s, but was still one of the most respected voices in science and technology throughout the world. When he went to Paris to lecture, people listened, and suddenly French aviators were distressed to learn of the Wright brothers' success.

Speaking to the French Aero-Club, Chanute made it sound as if the Wright brothers were his prodigies: "Admitting that he was no longer very young, he [Chanute] took pains to train young, intelligent, and daring pupils, capable of carrying on his research by multiplying his gliding experiments to infinity."[28] It was bad enough that Chanute made it seem that the brothers were his pupils, but he also revealed some of the reasons for their successes in 1902. He explained the theory of wing warping; he described how the operator lay in a cradle instead of standing up as Lilienthal had done; and he practically gave away the physical dimensions of the new 1903 craft.

It is a wonder that the Wright–Chanute relationship continued after his lecture in Paris. Perhaps the two brothers, who were polite to a fault, thought the old man had simply misunderstood them. Surely, he did not mean to give away their secrets. At least Chanute had not revealed the location of their tests, saying only that they were over a sandy area, and that the brothers had hardly suffered more than a pair of torn trousers in all their experiments. Because there would be no prying eyes, it was time to return to Kitty Hawk and Kill Devil Hills.

THE FLYING MACHINE

For the previous two years, Wilbur and Orville had called their different crafts "flying machines," but the appellation only really applied to the 1903 craft. They had disassembled their new flyer, packed it in crates, and had it sent to Kitty Hawk before they arrived in August 1903. Time was short: That same month, Langley launched his own flying machine.

Langley had, if anything, endured even more than the Wright brothers. He had begun to experiment with flight around 1890, years before them, and he had used all the resources at his disposal, including the workshops of the Smithsonian Museum. But everything came down to one major test: He had to launch his craft in front of an audience, so that the U.S. government would give him further funding.

He conducted two tests in the final months of 1903—one in October and the other in December. His powerful engine seemed to catapult the heavy aerodrome, as he called it, into

On December 8, 1903, Samuel Pierpont Langley attempted his second launch of a manned aircraft in the Potomac River. Unfortunately for Langley, his aerodrome fell into the water shortly after launch.

the air, but seconds later it fell into the Potomac River. It was a disappointment for Langley, made much worse by the reaction of the press. Newspapers such as the *New York Times* ridiculed his effort, and the idea that man simply was not meant to fly gained more support. It was against this backdrop that the Wrights began their final set of tests.

AUTUMN 1903

The work was demanding for the Wright brothers. Once in Kitty Hawk, Wilbur, Orville, and their friend George Spratt had to reassemble the flyer and rebuild their cabin as well. They had to experiment with different kinds of pulleys and tracks, because, without wheels, the flyer would never get off the ground without greasing the skids (part of the landing gear) in some way. Days passed, then weeks.

Learning of Langley's failure, Wilbur simply noted that it would be the brothers' turn next. The weather turned against them, though, first with punishing winds and then with bitter cold. Chanute arrived in October but spent little more than a week. This kind of roughing it was too much at his age. But during his short time with the brothers, Chanute seemed to put a damper on their plans. An accomplished engineer, Chanute doubted whether the brothers had taken into account the amount of power their engine and propellers would lose, leaving less than enough power for thrusting the plane forward. Chanute also attempted to do something that he had tried before. Ignoring the fact that the brothers had always worked on their own—and showed every intention of continuing to do so—he again offered to take them under his wing. They could concentrate on flying the gliders he was designing in Chicago. Orville wrote about it rather bitterly in a letter home: "He doesn't seem to think our machines are so much superior as the manner in which we handle them. We are of just the reverse opinion."[29] The Wrights had confidence in the calculations they had drawn up and in Charlie Taylor's engine. They were not sorry to see Chanute leave, but, as was often the case, they were also startled by his generosity. As he left North Carolina, Chanute purchased and sent warm winter gloves to the Wrights, who, as usual, were roughing it.

In addition to dealing with Chanute, the Wrights had other problems: there were a series of mechanical failures; sprockets had to be ordered; the engine had to be tinkered with; and the skids system had to be improved. One thing led to another, and before long it was the end of November. Around this time, one of the propeller shafts broke, and Orville had to leave camp. Moving very quickly, he went by train back to Dayton, and then turned around for his return trip. He got back on Friday, December 11. This was by far the latest the brothers had ever stayed at Kill Devil Hills, and the weather was testing them in a number of ways. Blowing sand was a constant hazard to the eyes, and bitter cold at night meant that a fire had to be kept going most of the time. The

Wrights were astonishingly resilient men, and they were steadfast in their quest. Raised by their formidable father, they had no time for lament, sorrow, or self-pity. They always forged ahead.

Orville's diary entry of Sunday, December 13, 1903, is most revealing of their upbringing: "Wind of 6 to 8 meters blowing from west and later from north. Air warm. Spent most of day reading. In afternoon Mr. Etheridge of L.S. Station, with wife and children, called to take a look at machine."[30] A wind of 6 to 8 meters would have been almost perfect, but, again, the brothers had promised their father never to work on a Sunday. They took the day to rest, even though they had been waiting for the right moment for days.

Finally it came: Thursday, December 17, 1903, was a day of strong but not excessive wind. Again, Orville's diary provides one of the best descriptions: "When we got up a wind of between 20 and 25 miles was blowing from the north. We got the machine out early and put out the signal for the men at the station."[31] Five men from the lifesaving station and one local teenager came to Kill Devil Hills. Bill Tate, who had first greeted the Wright brothers three years before, slept in that morning because he was sure the brothers would not try to fly in so strong a wind.

This time the Wrights did not use an incline. They wanted to be the first men to achieve unaided flight, under the flyer's own power, starting from a level surface. A famous photograph, perhaps the most famous from all aerial history, shows Wilbur running on the right side of the flyer at the moment it took off. (Orville was in the cradle, at the controls). Here, in the words of the operator, is the first flight:

> The machine lifted from the truck just as it was entering on the fourth rail. Mr. Daniels took a picture just as it left the tracks. I found the control of the front rudder quite difficult on account of its being balanced too near the center and thus had a tendency to turn itself when started. . . . Time about 12 seconds.[32]

On December 17, 1903, Orville and Wilbur Wright launched the first manned flight in Kitty Hawk, North Carolina. At 10:35 A.M., Orville took to the air and covered 120 feet in 12 seconds.

FOLLOW-UP AND EXPANSION

Wilbur and Orville knew they had done it. Four years of excruciating trial and error had paid off as Orville glided above the ground. But they wanted to do more, to show the men from the lifesaving station just how important this was. They wanted those men to be able to serve as witnesses.

Wilbur took the controls for the second flight. He covered about 175 feet. Then Orville went up for the third flight. He took the craft higher than on any previous flight or glide. Then, at almost precisely 12:00 P.M., Wilbur went up for his second time.

The machine started off with its ups and downs as it had before, but by the time he had gone over three or four hundred feet he had it under much better control, and was traveling on a fairly even course. It proceeded in this manner till it reached a small hummock about 800 feet from the starting ways.[33]

Wilbur Wright had flown a total of 59 seconds and covered 852 feet. There is no way to know his feelings at that moment, or those he had later that day. He had to be bursting with pride, but it was one tempered by humility. He, of all people, knew how difficult it had been to get to this point. He, of all fliers and would-be fliers, knew that this was only the beginning of what would be an even longer journey, one that would allow men and women to cover the skies with ease.

The Wrights' flyer did not survive the afternoon. Just minutes after Wilbur's stunning 59-second flight, the flyer, which had been sitting on the ground, was upended by a major gust of wind. Wilbur and one of the lifesaving men tried to rescue it, but to no avail. The magnificent craft that brought man into the sky had flown for the last time.

That night, Orville sent a telegram to their father: "Success four flights Thursday morning all against twenty one mile wind started from level with engine power alone average speed through air thirty one miles longest 59 seconds inform Press home Christmas."[34]

The telegraph operator in Norfolk, Virginia, was impressed enough to spread the news (even though the brothers asked him not to). There were articles in a number of newspapers during the next few days, but none back home in Dayton, Ohio. By all accounts, the local newspaper editor leaned back in his chair and said, "Fifty-nine seconds? If it had been fifty-nine minutes, then it *might* have been a news item."[35] This type of ignorance and dismissal would plague the Wrights for years to come.

The Prairie

Sometimes a picture really is worth a thousand words: In the spring of 1904, just six months after their stunning success at Kill Devil Hills in Kitty Hawk, North Carolina, the Wright brothers stood in front of their newly designed plane. In the picture, the plane is largely outside the hangar they had built, and it is plain to see that the brothers have come a long way in the past year or two. The propellers are clearly visible, and the shape looks much more like what we today would call an airplane (the word still had not yet been coined).

In the photo, Orville leans against the plane with his arms folded. His expression is serious, but not nearly as much as his brother's. Wilbur stands sideways to the camera, with a wrench in his left hand. His shoulders are slightly slumped, the smallest admission of fatigue, but there is an ironlike quality about his physique. Here is a man who will do whatever is necessary.

After they made history in December 1903, Wilbur and Orville Wright continued to perfect their aircraft, building a new flyer in the spring of 1904. Here, Orville leans against their new plane, while Wilbur stands sideways to the camera with a wrench in his hand.

Missing from the picture is mechanic Charlie Taylor, who in all likelihood was at the Wright Cycle Company, either serving a customer or working on another piece of metal or wood for the 1904 flyer.

PROPHETS WITHOUT HONOR

Wilbur and Orville did not expect the world to acknowledge their accomplishments right away, but they were still surprised by the attitude of the American press. The Norfolk telegraph operator did spill the beans, leaking Orville's famous telegram to other newspapers, but it was generally ignored by the press.

This response reveals two points: One, the American newspapermen were weary of stories of flight. The stupendous crashes of Langley's aerodrome had soured them temporarily on the idea that manned flight could be accomplished. Two, and just as important, the newsmen truly did not understand what the Wright brothers had done and were doing. Few people had extensive scientific knowledge in those days, and many of the newspapermen may well have mistaken Wilbur and Orville's claim that they flew for 59 seconds to have taken place in a type of *balloon*. If that was the case, 59 seconds would indeed not have been newsworthy.

However there were advantages to being unseen and unnoticed by the press. The Wrights and Taylor worked hard that winter, developing the new flyer and coming up with a new place to test it. A return to Kitty Hawk was out of the question. Though the brothers had liked the area, it was far too remote; they could not afford to waste time sending materials to Dayton for repair. They had to have Taylor on hand, so he could make, fix, and perfect the pieces of their flying machine. Also, they realized the sands of Kitty Hawk were harmful to the engine. Therefore, they looked around their local area and settled on a grassy place called Huffman Prairie, eight miles outside of Dayton.

Orville knew the area; he had gone there on a high school field trip. Teachers and professors alike were fond of pointing out that Huffman Prairie was one of the small pieces of true prairie that still existed in Ohio. Examining the spot, Wilbur and Orville found it far from ideal. The Dayton–Springfield train ran close by; the field was very small compared to what they were used to; and the humidity was stifling. They settled down to work just the same.

Dayton banker Torrance Huffman let the brothers use the field rent free, as long as they corralled his animals and made sure they came to no harm. Huffman did not outwardly support the brothers; privately he confessed he believed that they were crazy to persist with this flying machine. But, with the field theirs, the brothers went to work.

Perhaps it is fair to say that at this point the brothers truly became equal partners. The original conceptions of 1899 and the drive behind the glides of 1900 and 1901 had been all Wilbur's, but by 1904, the brothers were acting like one. From this point on, it becomes much more difficult to say which was Wilbur's idea or which was Orville's. They were joined in this all-consuming task.

On May 25, 1904, the brothers asked members of the local press to come to Huffman Prairie to see their first flights of the season. Not only did the newsmen show up; so, too, did old Bishop Wright, sister Katharine, and several other family members. They all came for what turned out to be one of the most dismal performances the Wrights gave.

Nothing worked that day. The wind did not cooperate and neither did the flatboards the brothers used to try to launch the flyer. Wilbur made one effort late in the day, and it did not work. The newsmen shook their heads and left. It would be a while before they would be convinced to come back to Huffman Prairie. Yet, once again, this may have been a blessing, for the Wrights had to contend with difficulties they had not experienced in the past.

THE TRIALS OF SUMMER

The area around Dayton, Ohio, is fairly flat and the weather is usually hot and humid in the summer. The brothers sweltered that summer, always wearing the long shirts, long pants, and hats that were their trademark. They thought it disrespectful to wear anything less formal. They tinkered with the flyer and sent messages back and forth to Taylor, but got in very little flying because the weather would not cooperate. The brothers were masters at watching the prairie grass, and, if there was a slight breeze, they would be up and at it, trying to start the machine. But the wind died down just as quickly. Many years later it was discovered that Huffman Prairie, though only 800 feet above sea level, had an extremely different wind pattern than Kitty

Hawk because of the humidity. Much of the summer was spent in quiet frustration.

FLYING IN THE MIDWEST

The Wrights found that it was challenging to fly at Huffman Prairie. The difference in the air conditions threw them off for most of the 1904 season. Ironically, however, aviators of the next generation or two often described the conditions in the Midwest as most agreeable.

Few people have ever described flying as well, or as eloquently, as Guy Murchie. In 1954, he published *Song of the Sky*, which describes the difference between flying in the Chinook wind current over the Rocky Mountains, in a waterspout over the Gulf of Mexico, and in the Santa Ana wind current over the desert Southwest. Here is what he had to say about the Midwest, home of the Wright brothers:

> The easiest country of all to fly is probably the flat American Midwest where not only can you land in almost any field if necessary but the section lines laid off in roads on the earth are a living page from a geography book, actual latitude and longitude lines breathing there beneath you. The farms were surveyed on the exact dimensions of the quarter section, 160 acres, the historic pioneer homestead. It is a true-life blueprint based on the equator and the Greenwich meridian, a plan of living drawn first on paper, second on the earth.[36]

The Wrights did not fly high enough—in 1904 and 1905—to take advantage of these geographic lines, but those who came after them certainly did.

The brothers were confident that their success in December 1903 put them far ahead of any competitors, but if news should spread, and if someone should manage to copy their wing-warping techniques, all might be lost. By this time, the brothers had firmly decided to make their fortune from the business of flight, but their flyer was not yet protected by patent—the U.S. Patent Office had rejected their first attempt, in 1903. The brothers had a right to be anxious. The competition was gaining on them, and most of the developments were in France.

Almost as soon as Octave Chanute had given his talk in Paris in 1903, a major movement started to develop. Patriotic Frenchmen were appalled that Americans were learning French secrets of flight, which they considered their domain. Later, when Chanute sent photographs of the 1902 glides with Wilbur at the helm, it was apparent that the Wrights were truly steering in the air; something no one else had ever done. Upset over being beaten to the chase, French aviators redoubled their efforts. Without knowing the full "hows" and "whys," they started to experiment with wing warping.

Meanwhile, Chanute pressed the brothers to enter the flight competition at St. Louis, Missouri. The World's Fair had been planned for St. Louis in 1903, but circumstances had interfered, and the competition was pushed back an entire year. The Wright brothers did travel to St. Louis during the winter of 1903–04, but they were not impressed by the field there. It seemed to favor balloons, so they decided not to participate. As usual, Wilbur was polite in his reply to Chanute:

> We have about concluded to enter the St. Louis contest but are reluctant to do so formally, until we are certain of being ready in time. We have one machine finished, another approaching completion, and a third well started. As these are built to measure, the parts are interchangeable, and even a rather serious accident would not necessarily throw us out of the contest. . . . It is true that the tortoise beat the hare in a great historic race, but if the hare can open its eyes a little sooner next time or keep from breaking its legs or neck, it might turn the tables on the tortoise next time in a rather surprising way.[37]

In 1904, the Wright brothers were invited to attend the World's Fair in St. Louis, Missouri, to demonstrate their aircraft. However, after inspecting the field they would be taking off from, they decided that the setup favored balloons, such as the California Arrow blimp, which is pictured here.

The Wrights did not go to St. Louis. They stayed at Huffman Prairie, dealing with the setbacks and disappointments.

AUTUMN GUSTS

The coming of autumn was fortuitous for the Wrights. Ever so slowly, the winds began to increase, and the air became lighter and drier. Day by day, they made small flights, ever watchful of nearby telephone wires.

As mentioned in Chapter 1, the Wrights were friends with Amos I. Root, who observed the first complete circle ever flown.

ALBERTO SANTOS-DUMONT
(1873–1932)

First Around the Eiffel Tower

The Wright brothers accomplished much during their aviation careers, but they went about it in a quiet way. At the other end of the spectrum was Brazilian aviator Alberto Santos-Dumont, who made a name for himself by flying dirigibles (balloons).

Santos-Dumont was born in Brazil in 1873 and was the son of one of the country's richest coffee growers. Like Wilbur Wright, Santos-Dumont was fascinated by the movements of birds, and he spent many hours observing them under the Brazilian sky. But, in 1891, the family moved to Europe, and Santos-Dumont settled in Paris, the home of the original hot-air balloon. Blessed to have received a large part of the family fortune, he was able to hire experts to instruct him on balloon flight and then to pioneer new ways on his own. By 1900, he had achieved real success in steering his balloons. That year, he accepted a challenge to compete for a 100,000-franc prize.

At the turn of the twentieth century, the Eiffel Tower was not yet beloved by Parisians. The tower had been erected for the 1889 World's Fair in Paris, but city dwellers still viewed the enormous metal structure with disgust and annoyance. Santos-Dumont helped popularize it through his efforts at flight. On October 19, 1901, he flew from Paris's Air Club to the Eiffel Tower and back in 30 minutes and 40 seconds, just a little longer than what was required to receive the prize. Parisians demanded that the money be given to him anyway, and Santos-Dumont ended up giving most of his winnings to the poor.

In the spring of 1904, Santos-Dumont brought his balloons to St. Louis to compete for the $100,000 prize at the World's Fair. A true celebrity by this time, he was favored to win, but someone sneaked into his workshop and sabotaged his craft. Angry over the destruction and over rumors that he had done it himself to avoid competing, Santos-Dumont went home to Paris.

Wilbur had made a half circle about two weeks before that, but no one was sure he could fly a 360-degree one until he accomplished the feat on September 20, 1904. From then on, the Wrights built on their accomplishments. Wilbur and Orville both made numerous flights in November and early December; on one memorable flight, Orville traveled a total of 11 miles. Wilbur gave a thorough report in a letter to Octave Chanute:

> During the season one hundred and five starts were made. The best flights since my last letter were on November 16th and December 1st, the flights being 2 and a quarter turns of the field on the first named date and almost four rounds on the last. . . . We saw our attorneys a few days after writing you and found that none of the references cited were of any serious importance. . . . We think the patents will be allowed, though in Germany it will be necessary to take out separate patents for the various features.[38]

1905

The year 1905 was less dramatic for the Wrights. By that time, they had accumulated far more scientific data than anyone else in the field. They felt confident in their ability to design, build, and fly airplanes, and now they wanted to earn profits from their work. Up to this point, they had not made a penny from the enterprise.

The trouble, as they well knew, was that the public, and perhaps the U.S. government, had become deeply skeptical over most claims to flight. The failure of Langley's aerodrome and other such failures led many people to dismiss all claims of heavier-than-air flight. Knowing that they would have to prove themselves, the Wrights went to their local Congressman. He readily agreed to ask U.S. Secretary of War William Howard Taft to look into the matter, but the letter was quickly passed on to the "experts," including those at the Smithsonian. The Wrights received a dismal rejection from the U.S. government:

> As many requests have been made for financial assistance
> . . . the device must have been brought to the stage of
> practical operation without expense of the United States.
> It appears from the letter of Messrs. Wilbur and Orville
> Wright that their machine has not yet been brought to
> the stage of practical operation.[39]

This was maddening to the brothers. They were not asking for financial assistance; they were looking for someone to purchase the planes they had made and flown. Had the brothers been willing to explain this in another letter, they may have received a different response. But there was a stubborn self-righteousness to the brothers in matters like this. If the U.S. government could not, or would not, recognize the benefit of an airplane, then they would look to other potential buyers.

Only three countries had the money and the willingness at the time to purchase the Wrights' airplane: Great Britain, France, and Germany. The brothers recognized that these three nations were all involved in a major arms race, which would ultimately lead to World War I a decade later. They were comforted with the notion that airplanes might make warfare obsolete—if a government or an army had the ability to send up planes that could identify everything about their foe, then they would not want to start a war in the first place. Or so the brothers hoped.

The Wrights continued to experiment in the summer and fall of 1905. Their 1905 Flyer was a marked improvement on the previous one, and they enjoyed much success in the air. On the ground, they dealth with a long series of delays and missteps in their attempt to interest foreign governments. At this time, Wilbur wrote to Chanute:

> We are not anticipating an immediate visit from the Britishers
> as we have had no word from them for several months and
> do not expect anything until we write or stir them up in some
> indirect way. We would prefer to finish up our experiments

for this season before they appear. We have never had any intention of showing the machine in advance of a definite understanding in regard to its purchase. We will give the American government another chance before finally accepting any foreign contract.[40]

What the Wrights did not foresee was that three years would pass before they would fly again.

The Bluffers

By the end of 1905, the Wrights were well ahead of schedule with their design and well behind in terms of finance. They knew that no one but a government could afford to give them the price they wanted for their airplanes, and none of the governments wanted to put up any money until they witnessed a flight. It was a perfect "Catch-22."

MORE COMPETITION

Samuel Langley suffered a paralyzing stroke in 1905. He rallied for a time, even returning to work in brief spurts. But he died just a few months later in February 1906, leaving the aeronautic field open to the Wrights and their new competitors.

Alexander Graham Bell gave Langley's eulogy. Bell expressed a good deal of bitterness toward the press, which had made Langley's life miserable after the two failed launches in the autumn of 1903. But instead of giving up the fight for the air, Bell and a new group of associates pressed ahead.

GLENN CURTISS
(1878–1930)

Innovator or Copycat?

Depending on one's point of view, Glenn Curtiss was either a brilliant innovator or a scoundrel. Born in Hammondsport, New York, in 1878, Curtiss had only an eighth-grade education, but that was typical for the time. His first job was with the Rochester, New York, firm that later became Eastman Kodak.

Curtiss started repairing bicycles and then moved to motorcycles. Some of his early work as a bicycle shop repairman resembled that of the Wrights, but he focused on power and speed, while they concentrated on balance and steering. Called the "hell rider" for the fast motorcycles he built, Curtiss attracted attention both for his antics and for his beautifully designed motors.

In 1907, at the urging of Alexander Graham Bell, Curtiss joined the Aerial Experiment Association (AEA). Curtiss worked with Bell's large kites but found them impractical. By 1908, Curtiss had designed the Red Wing and White Wing, aircraft that copied, but also improved upon, the wing-warping methods of the Wright brothers.

Curtiss's designs became known as ailerons, which accomplished wing warping without the need for cables and wires. The Wrights were incensed. To them it was a clear case of theft, but for Curtiss it was borrowing the ideas of another person and adapting them to a better purpose. The legal battles would go on for years.

Curtiss later turned to developing a plane that could land on water. He designed and built planes for the U.S. Navy during World War I. By the 1920s, he had become a real estate developer in Florida.

In 1907, the Wright brothers traveled to France for the first time to negotiate the sale of their aircraft with the French government. Although the government did not offer them a contract, they were able to sign on with a French company. Pictured here is Wilbur Wright (left) during the Wrights' second trip to France in 1909.

Ever since the late 1880s, Bell and his family had summered at the Bras d'Or Lake on Cape Breton Island in eastern Canada. Over the years, he expanded the original family house into a massive compound with lots of space to conduct experiments. Around the time of Langley's death, Bell was experimenting with massive kites and even circular objects that he thought offered greater stability in the air than anything the Wrights or anyone else had designed.

The truth was that Bell, despite all his brilliance, did not understand the many aspects of flight that the Wrights had perfected. For people like Bell, who never saw a Wright machine in flight, the whole idea seemed preposterous. Those like Amos I. Root, who did see a flyer in action, found it almost impossible to describe the event scientifically. None of these men were dim-witted, but they had a long way to go to catch up with the

Wrights. Bell might never have discovered wing warping if he had not become friends with Glenn Curtiss.

Bell, Curtiss, and others were in direct competition with the Wrights. They knew about the Wrights' designs and techniques, and it soon became a race to see which group would get to the finish line—financially speaking—first.

TRIP TO FRANCE

In May 1907, the same year that Bell and Curtiss experienced success for the first time, Wilbur crossed the Atlantic Ocean in a steamship for the first time. He went straight to Paris to begin negotiations with the French government regarding the flyer. There had been some interest in Germany, too, but a negative newspaper article spoiled it.

By the time he arrived, Paris was abuzz over new efforts made by Alberto Santos-Dumont and others. Motivated by the news that the Wrights had flown, a number of French aviators had designed better balloons and some very primitive planes. Parisians were thrilled to see one such plane lift and fly for a few meters, but there was no wing warping, and therefore no control.

Wilbur purposely declined to comment on anyone else's flying machines, pointing out the obvious—that any mechanic or inventor naturally thought his design was the best. Wilbur and Orville (who joined his brother in July) did not fly on this trip; their time was spent meeting French and German cabinet officers, the French president, and even the crown prince of Germany. There was no doubt the Wrights had become genuine celebrities, but the press wanted more information—about their planes, their plans, and themselves. Much of this interest was thwarted in the first Wright brothers' trip, and some, in the French press especially, began calling them *les bluffeurs* ("the bluffers"). After all, the Wrights had not conducted a single flight where any European could see them.

By this time, the Wrights were increasingly at odds with their friend Octave Chanute. Back in 1900, when Wilbur had first written to Chanute, the Frenchman had expressed his idea that there was little money to be made from aircraft innovation because the breakthroughs would probably come as a result of a combination of efforts. Chanute still adhered to this theory; it had always been his policy to circulate information as much as possible. But the brothers had become increasingly tight-lipped.

There were also difficulties in the negotiations with the foreign governments. The Wrights had signed an option agreement with the French government in 1906, but given the success of their own aviators, the French seemed disinclined to follow through. During this time, Orville wrote to his brother from Dayton:

> I was not in favor of taking up the business in France anyway, until we had seen what the Flints [the Wrights' agents in Europe] could do in new fields. I did not care to have them come in after we had some prospects there, which they had in no ways created, in order to get something at the last minute to continue our contract with them beyond September.[41]

Also during this time, Wilbur was promoting the use of the plane for intelligence gathering during times of war:

> But the flying machine has still another advantage of the greater importance. It is so small and inconspicuous, and moves so fast, that it is safe from the shots of the enemy at comparatively short distances. It comes and goes before the gunners can train their pieces and get the range. . . . But the enormous airship with its slow motion . . . cannot safely approach nearer than 3,000 yards, at which distance observations are of no military value.[42]

What had once been a game between two brothers was now becoming an international competition, with all the major powers hoping to use planes or balloons for military purposes.

TRIUMPHS

Orville and Katharine crossed the Atlantic late that summer to join Wilbur. He remained in Paris while they went on to Berlin.

The Wrights were in regular communication with the British, French, and German governments. Even U.S. government officials became convinced that they should negotiate with the Wright brothers. Contracts were signed, but the Wrights would not obtain any actual money until they performed some flights.

Three years had passed since they had last flown. Could they still do it? The Wrights never showed any concern, but their friends certainly did. Their father never wanted the brothers to fly in the same airplane, because any sort of accident could prove catastrophic for the family. Their financial backers were concerned that the Wrights might not turn in a great show and that all the negotiations would be in vain. They need not have worried. The meticulous approach to detail that had characterized the Wrights from the very beginning was still there.

RETURN TO KITTY HAWK

More than five years had passed since the brothers had accomplished their first flight. Now, in the spring of 1908, they returned to Kitty Hawk for some practice.

They found the town and people almost exactly the same. However, the condition of their buildings was another matter. Sand, wind, and water had all taken their toll. As before, the Wrights had to spend a good deal of time making their camp livable before they could fly. But once they went up in the air, their own doubts (unexpressed to others) were silenced.

They improved upon all their previous records at flight. They flew with better control than ever before. Their last flights before this had been at Huffman Prairie and they were relieved that they did not have to deal with high humidity or increased altitude. Bishop Wright confided in his diary that several

In 1908, the Wright brothers returned to Kitty Hawk to find their camp badly damaged. The elements had taken their toll on the Wrights' hangar: In this photo taken at the time of Wilbur's arrival on April 10 of that year, the roof has been blown off and the north wall has collapsed.

newspapers contained stories saying that the Wright brothers had flown 3,000 feet high and for 30 miles in one direction. If so, this surpassed any flights of the time.

FRANCE, 1908

In late May 1908, Wilbur sailed from New York on the *Touraine*. He knew France from his previous trip and from extensive reading over the years. An avid sightseer, he moved around Paris and the vicinity to visit cathedrals, towns, and the sites of great battles. He mixed this pleasure with business and reported to Orville:

> Our position is improving rapidly as it always does when one of us is here to meet people and infuse a little confidence in them. At first there was a tendency of the French papers to

be hostile, but I think it is about over. A similar tendency
among the leading aeronautical & automobile people seems
to be melting away too.[43]

Wilbur was in for a rude surprise, however. Early in June, he
opened the large crates and boxes in which Orville had shipped
the parts of the flyer, only to find they were damaged, although
not ruined. Wilbur scolded Orville from across the Atlantic,
but the carelessness was the fault of some packers in Elizabeth
City, North Carolina. Knowing that Orville had to be ready to
do his own flying—in front of members of the U.S. government—Wilbur let the matter drop and got down to business.

He found there was much to do. First he reassembled the
flyer. Its specifications had indeed changed over the years; it
was far larger than earlier Wright planes, but also far more
maneuverable. Then he looked for a suitable testing ground.
There were problems with the first two sites he looked at, but
eventually he found a better one at Le Mans, 30 miles outside
Paris. During this time, Wilbur also had to overcome an injury.
In July, he scalded himself badly, injuring his left side and arm.
Days passed before he could get back to work. He wrote to
Chanute, saying that Le Mans lacked many modern amenities,
much like Kitty Hawk, and that if he had known how hard
it would be to obtain mechanical assistance, he would have
brought a mechanic from the United States.

Photographs from this time show a very different Wilbur
than in earlier years. He was only 41 in 1908, but he looks far
older in the photographs because of his dour expression. He
had abandoned the high collars and starched shirts of earlier
days for an airman's black suit and gloves, and, given his frown
and the darkness of his apparel, there was something quite
grim about him.

Yet at the same time, the French began to accept him. Newsmen spent hours watching him and came away impressed with
his focus. He left not a single issue to assistants, but worked

constantly, and needed to test every pulley, line, and socket at least three times. Newspapers ran cartoons of Wilbur. They often portrayed him with a wry grin, but the bald head and vigorous stance were undeniably his. Children began to talk about "Monsieur Wright" and "les freres Wright" on a regular basis. Wilbur was, almost against his will, becoming a folk hero.

He saved his best for August. On August 10, Wilbur made two short flights at Le Mans. He made a figure eight on the second flight and came back to his starting point, much like a bird. The newspapers and the French aviators nearly went wild with excitement:

> [The French aviators Louis] Bleriot & [Ferdinand Léon] Delagrange were so excited they could scarcely speak, and [Henry] Kapferer could only gasp and not talk at all. You would have almost died of laughter if you could have seen them. The French newspapers, *Matin, Journal, Figaro, L'Auto, Petit Journal, Petit Parisien* … give reports fully as favorable as the *Herald*.[44]

Wilbur had done it. All skepticism about the Wright brothers, in France at least, had been dispelled.

VIRGINIA, 1908

At almost the same time, Orville was preparing to demonstrate a flyer to the U.S. Army. Negotiations between the Wrights and the U.S. government had yielded a very specific contract. The U.S. Army would purchase a Wright Flyer for $25,000 (far lower than what the Wrights wanted) if Orville could manage a flight carrying two persons with a combined weight of 350 pounds.

Orville arrived at Washington, D.C., in August 1908. He stayed at a hotel on Lafayette Square, very close to the White House; this was the first time one of the Wrights had been close to the center of power in the United States. Theodore Roosevelt was in the final year of his second term as president, but the most important person at the aerial demonstration was Vice President William Howard Taft. There were many leaders from the U.S. Army in attendance, including a signal corps officer whom Orville disliked intensely.

That officer was Lieutenant Thomas Selfridge, a flier himself. He was a member of the group Alexander Graham Bell had brought together in 1907, and he had piloted a short flight in one of the planes designed by Glenn Curtiss. Selfridge represented the U.S. Army at Fort Myer, Virginia, the location of the Wrights' presentation. But one could say he had a conflict of interest, because he was a competitor of the Wrights.

Orville made his first flight on September 3 without a hitch. He flew as high as the army required. But there was still the matter of carrying a second passenger. And so Orville and Lieutenant Selfridge went up on September 18. The photographs from the time are revealing in many ways: Selfridge looks grim as they prepare to take off. For his part, Orville had written an extremely revealing letter to Wilbur on September 6, saying, "I will be glad to have Selfridge out of the way. I don't trust him an inch. He is intensely interested in the subject, and plans to meet me often at dinners, etc., where he can try to pump me. He has a good education and a clear mind. I understand that he does a good deal of knocking [me] behind my back."[45]

Soon after they were in the air on September 18, Orville had to cut his engine. A propeller blade had broken; it would have thrashed about, perhaps wrecking the motor. The plane turned down in its front section and began to plummet.

Modern aviation had its first casualty. Lieutenant Selfridge was killed instantly, but Orville was hauled away from the wreckage. He had survived a number of crashes in the past, but nothing like this. Katharine Wright, on learning the news, took

On September 17, 1908, Orville Wright and Lieutenant Thomas Selfridge, who was onboard as an official observer, took off from Virginia's Fort Myer in one of the Wrights' flyers. Tragically, Selfridge was killed when the flyer crashed due to a damaged propeller.

a leave of absence from her teaching job and rushed to Virginia. She wrote home to their older brother Lorin:

> I found Orville looking pretty badly. His face is cut in several places, the deepest gash being over his left eye. His leg had just been set, yesterday afternoon. He was looking for me, and when I went in his chin quivered and the tears came to his eyes, but he soon braced up again. . . . The only time that he showed any sign of breaking up was when he asked me if I knew that Lieutenant Selfridge was dead.[46]

Lady Liberty
and Grant's Tomb

By 1908, the year Wilbur flew at Le Mans and Orville crashed at Fort Myer, New York City had become the unofficial capital of the United States. Of course, Washington, D.C., was the actual capital, but New York had become the most prominent city.

The first skyscrapers had been built in the 1880s and were followed by so many that Manhattan was soon recognizable by its unique skyline. Hundreds of ships crowded New York Harbor every day. Hundreds of thousands, if not millions, of people went to work each day, making Manhattan the greatest beehive of activity in North America. London still surpassed New York City in overall wealth, especially in finance and insurance, but a careful observer could foretell that New York would eventually overtake London.

This was the city that Wilbur Wright came to conquer in 1909.

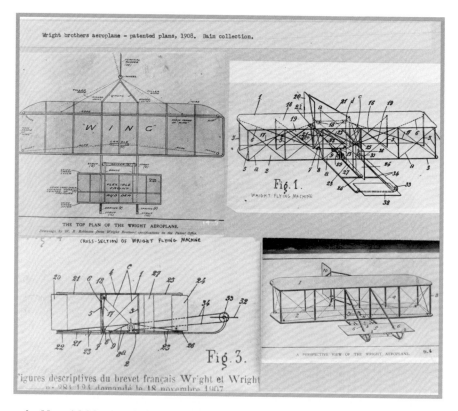

In May 1906, the Wright brothers were granted a patent in the United States for the "flying machine," and within the next few years, they received patents for it in five more countries. Pictured here are the specifications for their aeroplane, which were drawn in 1908.

RECOVERY

The Wrights had a bad scare in 1908. Orville's injuries were serious, and though he recovered, he would be bothered by chronic pain for the rest of his life.

Their reputation had suffered a bit, too. No one overtly blamed the Wrights for the plane crash, and the U.S. Army did fulfill its contract to purchase a Wright Flyer, but people continued to talk about the bad blood between the Wright brothers and Glenn Curtiss. Of course it was absurd to accuse

Orville of wanting to harm Lieutenant Selfridge (when he was so badly hurt himself), but people still gossiped.

By 1909, the Wrights' financial future had been secured. They would always have enough money, given that both the French and U.S. governments now wanted to buy their planes. But the Wrights also wanted to extend their patents (they had them in six countries) to all aspects of wing warping, thereby ensuring that no one else could ever profit from the discoveries they had made.

By this time, Wilbur and Orville were ready to hang up their aviator's caps. Orville's accident at Fort Myer was proof positive of the dangers of flying. But to ensure the success of their contracts and patents, they decided to focus on a series of flights that would be the last of their careers.

Orville and Katharine left for France at the start of 1909. She had become his nurse, the person on whom he leaned. She had left her teaching position for good and would continue to be his caretaker for many years. They landed in France and met with Wilbur, who had been continuing his work there during the past few years. Only upon arriving in France did Orville and Katharine learn that their brother's actions had made the Wrights famous.

Even though he knew what had happened to Orville at Fort Myer, Wilbur had pressed ahead. During the autumn of 1908, he had moved his exhibition from Le Mans to Pau, in southwestern France, where the weather was more agreeable. Pau also attracted more important European leaders, including royalty. King Alphonso of Portugal came to speak with Wilbur and to sit in a Wright Flyer, though he did not go up in the air.

Katharine Wright was an immediate hit with the European press. Her handsome features and natural charm endeared her to many, and her knowledge of several languages helped, too. Some called her the "perfect" American woman. She also became the first woman of any nation to fly in a plane, with Wilbur naturally at the controls.

By midsummer 1909, the Wrights had made their plans. Wilbur and Katharine would return home while Orville would stay in Europe to fly at a major exhibition that fall. Once again, the brothers would fly at similar times, more than 3,000 miles apart, and once again the stakes were high.

HUDSON-FULTON EXHIBITION

The year 1909 was the three hundredth anniversary of explorer Henry Hudson's discovery of the river that now bears his name. It was also the one hundredth anniversary of Robert Fulton piloting the *Clermont* up the Hudson River from Manhattan to Albany. New York City officials wanted the 1909 Hudson-Fulton Exhibition to be a gala celebration, complete with visiting ships from foreign nations, fireworks, and, of course, some spectacular flights by airplanes.

The Wrights knew they had made a mistake by not entering the competition at the 1904 World's Fair in St. Louis, Missouri. Determined not to repeat the mistake, Wilbur traveled to Governors Island, just off the tip of Manhattan, in early September.

The American press had taken a long time to warm up to the Wright brothers, but they made a great fuss over Wilbur that autumn. Within days of his arrival, he was interviewed by the *New York Times*, which just a few years earlier had held the general opinion that man was not intended to fly.

Shortly before his flight, Wilbur was asked about the conditions on Governors Island:

> This is better than any aerodome I have ever had, and it's simply incomparable with Fort Myer. The area available there was not much bigger than the old parade ground here. I don't think it has ever been realized what wonderful flying my brother Orville did there.[47]

Wilbur made every effort to refer to Orville when he met the press, but one still had the impression that he was the senior partner, giving pats on the back to the junior one. The *Times* then asked Wilbur about the danger of a flight over and around Manhattan. Was he not concerned with the drafts that would come up from the skyscrapers, as well as the hundreds of ships in the harbor?

> Well, all I would have to do would be to look out for a safe landing place on some large flat roof . . . The only real danger will be in striking the projecting edges of the buildings, but I feel that the machine could be safely manipulated as a glider to make a satisfactory landing. . . . If it comes, I will do my best to get out of it gracefully.[48]

Whether he meant to or not, Wilbur was helping to build the Wright legend. What other flier of the time would be so daring?

Only one: Glenn Curtiss.

Curtiss and the Wrights were serious competitors by this time. Orville had started legal proceedings against Curtiss for patent infringement just a few weeks earlier. The question was whether Curtiss's use of ailerons (stiff, small wings) infringed on the Wrights' patent on wing warping.

Curtiss also entered the competition for the Hudson-Fulton Exhibition. He and Wilbur met each other, very casually, on Governors Island before the events started. They were cordial to each other, but those who knew Wilbur believed that he had his tongue curled inside his lip. He was always more effective fighting his legal battles on paper, than in public.

The press continued its questions. How high could a flyer go? How many miles could it cover? "Why, 500 miles, perhaps 1,000 miles," was Wilbur's quick answer. "It is simply a case of human endurance combined with the quantity of fuel that the machine is able to carry—I could carry from 200 to 300 pounds of gasoline, and that would take me a long distance."[49] Another question: Would Wilbur try to fly from Manhattan to Albany? Wilbur replied:

> There you go again! . . . That's why I say that newspaper publicity, stimulated as it is by the enormous pressure of the public demand for fresh sensations, has debauched the science of aviation. Too many of the men flying now are being led astray by the desire for notoriety. What we want now is not so much longer flights as more instructive flights.[50]

As much as one can sympathize with Wilbur's position, one has to conclude that there was no way to turn back the clock. Exhibition flying was here to stay.

THE FLIGHTS

Wilbur readied his plane on the morning of September 29. The Hudson-Fulton Exhibition was then in its fourth day. There was a canoe attached to the bottom of the plane, as a primitive kind of life preserver.

He lifted up in a 15-mile breeze and soon passed from Governors Island to the lower tip of Manhattan. Hundreds of thousands of people were watching, and, for most of them, this was the first real flight they had ever seen.

"He's going to do it!" shouted people in the crowd. Indeed, Wilbur was about to pass around the Statue of Liberty. No one had ever done this before; no one had even come close. For a minute, Wilbur disappeared from sight, then reemerged on the southern side of the Statue of Liberty. At that moment, as if it had been planned, the passenger ship *Lusitania* moved into sight. Viewers saw the old and the new meet each other in New York Harbor that day.

Coming down less than five minutes after he took off, Wilbur was heard to say to Charlie Taylor, "Goes pretty well, Charlie." The ever-faithful mechanic replied, "Looks all right

In September 1909, the Wright brothers solidified their reputation after Wilbur took off from Governors Island and circled the Statue of Liberty during a five-minute flight. As many as one million people witnessed Wilbur's flight that day, including these people, who have gathered around him after the flight.

to me, Will." Behind the remarkable nonchalance was a system the two had developed over the years. Everything had been checked, rechecked, and triple-checked before Wilbur ever lifted off. He had become a master at both the technical aspects of flight and the art of making it all look easy.[51]

LOUIS BLÉRIOT
(1872–1936)

The First Man to Fly
Across the English Channel

Proud of their aviation heritage, which dates back to the Montgolfier brothers of the 1780s, the French were dismayed that the Americans—the Wrights in particular—had achieved flight first. Undaunted, one Frenchman in particular, Louis Blériot, focused on building lightweight monoplanes and biplanes, including his Blériot V, which successfully achieved flight (though it crashed not soon after takeoff).

In 1909, the London *Daily Mail* offered a £1,000 prize to any pilot who could successfully fly across the English Channel. After setting a European endurance record for sustained flight earlier that year, when he flew for 36 minutes and 55 seconds, Blériot was confident that he could become the first aviator to cross the channel. On July 25, 1909, just weeks before Wilbur Wright flew around Manhattan, Blériot left from Les Barraques (near Calais), on the French side of the channel, and flew northwest-by-west in his Blériot XI. The English Channel is infamous for its inclement weather, and Blériot became lost for a time, but then he saw four steamships somewhere near the English coast. Following them, he made the 22-mile (35-kilometer) trip to Dover in 40 minutes to become the first man ever to fly across the English Channel.

Glenn Curtiss also made a flight that day, but it was nowhere near as spectacular. Wilbur had stolen the show.

A week later, at the beginning of October, Wilbur made an even more daring flight. There had been much talk of going completely around Manhattan Island, but no one had tried it yet. There were dozens, if not hundreds, of hazards, ranging from unpredictable wind currents, many of them caused by the flow of air through the buildings of the Manhattan skyline. Wilbur went ahead anyway.

Starting from Governors Island, he flew north-by-north-west all the way to Grant's Tomb on the northwest side of the island. Turning his craft, Wilbur flew down Manhattan's East Side, returning safely to Governors Island. This was, by far, the most sensational flight of Wilbur Wright's career. It was also his last. He would soon be grounded by the need to defend the Wrights' patents against infringement. But for the moment, he was New York's hero and America's, too.

Just days later, Wilbur received a visit at the Park Avenue Hotel from a young banker. Enthusiastic over the potential of what he had seen, this 24-year-old offered to put together a Wright Flying company. At the time, Wilbur was only 42, but the number of years between this 24-year-old and himself seemed immense. He agreed to the deal, however, and Clinton Peterkin showed himself as adept at finance as Wilbur was with planes. The Wright Company was formed just weeks later. Wilbur and Orville received a handsome cash payment, stock options for the future, and the promise that the new company would bear all their expenses in the defense of their patents.

Preserving the
Wright Legacy

Unfortunately for the Wrights, things went downhill rather quickly after the Manhattan success. This is not to say that the Wrights lost all the battles or that they were miserable. But fame and fortune exacted a high price on all the members of the Wright family.

Wilbur flew only one time after 1909 and that was as a passenger. Perhaps he was weary of the constant checking and rechecking that an aviator had to do; or perhaps he had just decided that the danger was not worth it. But most of all, he was occupied with legal battles pertaining to who had the right to fly.

The Wrights obtained patents in a total of six countries, all of them to do with the concept of wing warping. According to the language of the patent, the Wrights should therefore receive a royalty each and every time someone made or sold a plane using that technique. The problem was that by 1910, Glenn Curtiss and others had moved beyond wing warping. They used the basic concept, but they improved on it with the construction of ailerons, which were stiffer, sturdier, and required the pilot to use fewer controls. According to Glenn Curtiss and others, they had moved past wing warping and therefore had no reason to pay the Wright brothers.

To say there were hard feelings between the Wrights and Curtiss is an understatement. There was anger, bitterness, and, at times, real hatred. Katharine Wright, famed for her grace and hospitality, loathed Curtiss so much she could hardly mention his name without venom.

All along, Wilbur and Orville had desired to avoid legal battles, but once the process began, they could not resist fighting for what they believed was rightfully theirs. They went to court a number of times in 1910 and 1911, each round of legal battles taking some of the brothers' strength. There was plenty of fight in the Wrights, but they were increasingly weary of the whole affair.

Glenn Curtiss, by contrast, was up for the challenge and thought he had a perfectly good case. The Wrights might have prevailed early on if Curtiss had not been assisted by another inventor, Henry Ford. The automobile pioneer sympathized with Curtiss, for he had fought a similar patent battle with inventor George Selden. Ford lent money and expertise to Curtiss, but the Wrights still prevailed. The irony was that by the time the Wrights won in court, their own company was starting to use the very ailerons that Curtiss and his company had pioneered.

Though the Wrights won most of the legal battles, they started to lose a public relations war and some of their old friends as well. The first and biggest casualty was their relationship with Octave Chanute. Truthfully, there had long been disagreements between the brothers and their good friend, but both sides had managed to avoid a serious conflict. The brothers' bad feelings toward Chanute dated back to 1903, when he revealed some of their secrets to a French audience, and then when he had the audacity to suggest they give up their experiments and work for him. Chanute's bad feelings are not as well documented, but there had been times over the years when he had read newspaper accounts stating that the Wright brothers were indebted to no one in their pursuit of flight. Chanute felt this was going too far and said so. At the time, the brothers were able to account for this statement by saying that they meant they were *financially* indebted to no one. But in 1910, Chanute was interviewed by the *New York World* and stated:

> I admire the Wrights. I feel friendly toward them for the marvels they have achieved; but you can easily gauge how I feel concerning their attitude at present by the remark I made to Wilbur Wright recently. I told him I was sorry to see they were suing other experimenters and abstaining from entering the contests and competitions in which other men are brilliantly winning laurels.[52]

Chanute went on to say that he doubted that the technique of wing warping could be patented because other people—as far back as the 1870s—had written about it. The *New York World* interview led to a short exchange of bitter letters between Wilbur and Chanute, with both men standing their ground. Wilbur was especially incensed because Chanute had implied that the Wrights were too concerned with making money. In a letter to Chanute, Wilbur wrote:

> As to inordinate desire for wealth, you are the only person acquainted with us who has ever made such an accusation. We believed that the physical and financial risks which we took, and the value of the service to the world, justified sufficient compensation to enable us to live modestly with

enough surplus income to permit the devotion of our future time to scientific experimenting instead of business.[53]

The crux of the problem was that Chanute always thought he was more important to the Wrights than they did. His pioneering book of 1894, *Progress in Flying Machines*, had greatly helped those who yearned to fly, and he often lent a helping hand to the Wrights, but the brothers had done the vast majority of the work alone. They had always chosen to go it alone whether in failure or success. Now, when they had reached the summit and wanted to cash in on their success, Chanute seemed to be in their way. Wilbur concluded the letter to Chanute by writing: "If anything can be done to straighten matters out to the satisfaction of both you and us, we are not only willing but anxious to do our part. There is no pleasure to us in the situation which has existed. . . . We have no wish to quarrel with a man toward whom we ought to preserve a feeling of gratitude."[54]

Chanute did not answer. Wilbur wrote again a month later, and Chanute sent a reply. He held open the possibility they might reconcile, but he died later that year.

STATUS

The Wrights had never seemed interested in money or creature comforts, but perhaps, like many people, they looked toward that direction as they grew older. In 1912, work began on a magnificent mansion located several miles from their longtime home in Dayton. Milton Wright longed for peace and happiness. He wanted to be surrounded by his family and for them to not worry about the fight over patents and rights. He and Katharine might well have persuaded the brothers to do this, but Wilbur became sick at the beginning of May 1912.

He had eaten a seafood dinner in Boston that didn't agree with him, and back in Dayton he was diagnosed with typhoid fever, the illness that Orville had barely survived back in the 1890s. That narrow escape from death had made the brothers

In 1912, Orville Wright began building a mansion in Dayton, Ohio, where his family could spend time together. The mansion was completed in 1914 and some members of the Wright family, including Orville (third from left), Milton (center), and Katharine (third from right), are pictured here in front of Orville's home.

exceptionally aware of typhus and vigilant in protecting their water from any contamination. But Wilbur was stricken just the same. He rallied a bit, and then succumbed to unconsciousness. He died on May 30, 1912.

Milton Wright wrote in his diary: "Wilbur is dead and buried! We are all stricken. It does not seem possible that he is gone. Probably Orville and Katharine felt his loss most. They say little. Many letters. Ezra Kuhns comes, reads Wilbur's will, and leaves copies. I ride 20 miles with Orville in auto."[55]

The world mourned, too. Thousands of flowers arrived from all parts of the United States. Tributes were in every newspaper and magazine. The *New York Times* displayed a typical photo of Wilbur, looking hardheaded and sure of himself. One of the finest tributes came from a French newspaper:

> Alone the man with the curious birdlike profile whom we saw at Le Mans in 1908 possessed the secret of flight in space. Since 1903, helped by his brother Orville, above the sands of North Carolina, he had experimented with the first mechanical bird, entirely conceived by his own mind; had built its wings, invented the motor that gave it artificial life, making it obey his will. It can be said that the world appropriated his secret. How deplorable, therefore, it is that even recently endeavors were made to deprive him of the benefit from an achievement due entirely to his genius.[56]

A year later, the family moved into the mansion, soon to be called Hawthorn Hill. From the outside the family looked prosperous and secure, but life in the new surroundings was never as comfortable or as happy as in the past. Wilbur had contributed something very special to the family. It would be unfair to the others to say that he was the pillar of the family, but he came close.

Orville did not stay in the aviation business for much longer. Professing that he had no desire for business (that had been Wilbur's forte), Orville sold all his interests in the Wright Company by 1915. He had plenty of money with which to enjoy his retirement. Orville tinkered with different mechanical devices over the years, but he never came close to any sort of big breakthrough such as he and Wilbur had enjoyed together.

Milton Wright died in 1917, at the age of 88. Nearly 10 years later, Katharine Wright passed away. At the age of 52, she told Orville she was leaving to marry a friend from her college

During his final years, Orville Wright became embroiled in a feud with the Smithsonian Institution over its claim that Samuel Pierpont Langley had constructed a machine that was capable of flight before the Wrights had constructed theirs. Orville is pictured here with a wind tunnel balance instrument in 1946, two years prior to his death.

days at Oberlin. Furious over what he felt was abandonment, Orville did not write or speak to her for the next two years. Only when he learned that she had contracted pneumonia and was close to death did he rush to her bedside. He was with her when she died.

Orville's last years—he died in 1948—were mysterious to outsiders. For a man who had shown such nerve and daring in pursuing the secrets of flight, he seemed to retreat into himself, showing little interest in anything except for nasty legal battles with the Smithsonian Institution. These squabbles became so bad that Orville sent the original 1903 Wright Flyer

CHARLIE TAYLOR
(1868–1956)

The Last of the Three

Charlie Taylor never asked anyone to feel sorry for him, but one can do so just the same. He was born in 1868 on an Illinois farm, one year after Wilbur. He moved to Indiana in his youth, and then migrated to Dayton, where his wife's family lived.

Taylor constructed the first engine ever to power a craft in the air, and for that he was indispensable to the Wright brothers for years afterward. He went with them to France in 1907. He was also there on the ground while Wilbur made his flight around the Statue of Liberty in New York in 1909. But Charlie fell on hard times soon after Wilbur's death.

He and his family spent many years in California, where his wife took ill, finally ending up in a hospital for the last decade of her life. Taylor bought a lot of desert land in southern California, which he hoped would prove prosperous, but the stock market crash of 1929 and the Great Depression that followed thwarted that hope. By 1936, he was broke and looking for work.

He worked for automaker Henry Ford for a while and helped move the former Wright Cycle Company, brick by brick, to Ford's new Greenfield Village in Dearborn, Michigan. When that work ended, Taylor went back to California, working on an assembly line during World War II. He later claimed that he matched the younger men, stride for stride. He suffered a heart attack in the summer of 1945 and had to leave work.

Taylor's last communication with the Wrights was in a December 1947 letter from Orville, who said he hoped Taylor was well and happy, but that knowing him, it was unlikely since he had little work to do.

Taylor died in January 1956. The man who had built the world's first flying motor was alone and penniless at the end.

to England to be displayed in a British museum, rather than the Smithsonian. But his reputation as being a recluse was not accurate. Those who knew Orville well thought he was quite happy in retirement; that he did not mind being away from the action of flight.

The quarrel with the Smithsonian was finally settled in the 1940s, but the Wright Flyer did not return to the United States until soon after Orville's death in 1948. By then, aviation had become unrecognizable from the Kitty Hawk days.

The first planes had been built on the two-decker system, first developed by Chanute and improved on by the Wrights. These planes had played a rather small part in World War I; they were used either as reconnaissance units or in combat. (Wilbur and Orville's dream that airplanes would reduce the likelihood of warfare did not come to fruition.)

Shortly after the war, in the 1920s, airplanes began to become more popular. For example, barnstorming—sensational flights done by traveling shows across the United States—became extremely popular. The first small-time mail delivery services began. But the event that truly launched aviation, making it the dream and desire of many, was Charles "Lucky" Lindbergh's flight in 1927.

At the time, he was only 25 and looked a bit awkward. Too young to fly in World War I, he started flying in 1923. In May 1927, he flew across the Atlantic Ocean alone, from Long Island to Paris, in 33 hours and 30 minutes. More than a hundred thousand Frenchmen greeted him with flowers, songs, and feelings of elation. Through the rest of his life—which was marked by difficulty and controversy as well as success—Lindbergh was the immortal "Lone Eagle," the first person to accomplish this flight alone. One might well ask: Could it have been Wilbur or Orville?

They certainly had the know-how and the intrepid spirit, but, even if Wilbur had not tragically died at 45, the odds are he would not have attempted such a flight. Flying was a young man's sport, he often said, and he would have been content to sit on the sidelines, knowing that his and his brother's work had made flight possible. By the time Orville died in 1948, the skies were growing thick with airplanes (the word had entered the English language in 1907). Even so, the aviators of that time might not have guessed that millions of people in the future would fly commercially and that air travel would quickly surpass train travel.

The Wrights did not accomplish all of this, but their actions made much of it possible. It is very likely that someone else would have accomplished what the Wrights did, but it might have taken a good deal longer. One has only to remember Wilbur's pessimistic words to Orville as they traveled back from Kitty Hawk in the autumn of 1901—that man would learn to fly, but it might take another hundred years.

Chronology

1859   Milton Wright marries Susan Koerner.

1861   Reuchlin Wright is born.

1862   Lorin Wright is born.

1867   Wilbur Wright is born.

1868   Charlie Taylor is born in Illinois.

1871   Orville Wright is born.

1874   Katharine Wright is born.

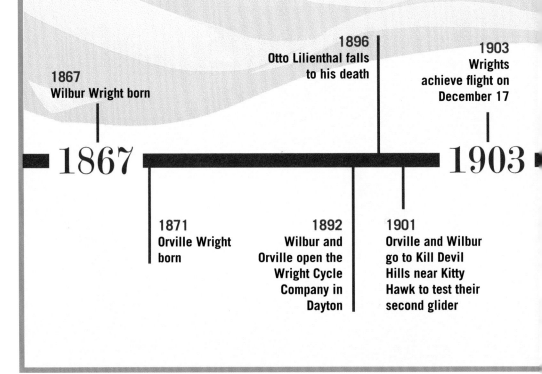

Timeline

1867
Wilbur Wright born

1896
Otto Lilienthal falls
to his death

1903
Wrights
achieve flight on
December 17

1867

1903

1871
Orville Wright
born

1892
Wilbur and
Orville open the
Wright Cycle
Company in
Dayton

1901
Orville and Wilbur
go to Kill Devil
Hills near Kitty
Hawk to test their
second glider

1889   Susan Koerner Wright dies.

1892   Wilbur and Orville open the Wright Cycle Company in Dayton.

1896   German glider Otto Lilienthal falls to his death.

1899   Wilbur begins corresponding with the Smithsonian Institution and working on problems of flight.

1900   Wilbur corresponds with Octave Chanute and later goes to Kitty Hawk with Orville.

1901   Orville and Wilbur go to Kill Devil Hills near Kitty Hawk, North Carolina, to test their second glider; Chanute and others visit the camp; later Wilbur speaks

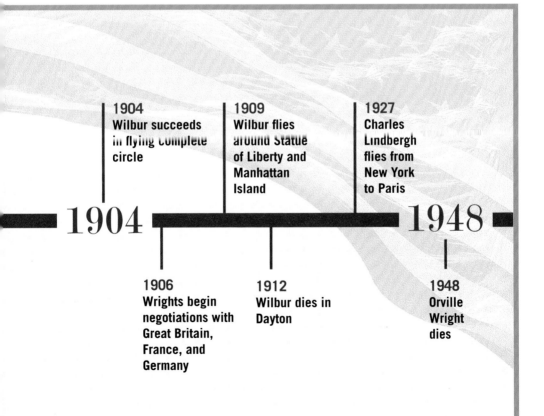

1904
Wilbur succeeds in flying complete circle

1909
Wilbur flies around Statue of Liberty and Manhattan Island

1927
Charles Lindbergh flies from New York to Paris

1904   1948

1906
Wrights begin negotiations with Great Britain, France, and Germany

1912
Wilbur dies in Dayton

1948
Orville Wright dies

at Chicago Society of Engineers; brothers experiment with wind tunnel.

1902   Wrights create new mathematical tables and new, improved glider; major successes in October.

1903   Chanute speaks to French engineers; Charlie Taylor builds engine and Wrights return to Kitty Hawk/Kill Devil Hills; Langley fails over Potomac River; Wrights end year with stunning success on December 17.

1904   Wrights perform tests of new glider at Huffman Prairie; Amos I. Root witnesses flight; Wilbur succeeds in flying complete circle; St. Louis Centennial flights take place.

1905   Wrights send letters to U.S., British, and French governments.

1906   Langley dies; Wrights begin negotiations with Great Britain, France, and Germany.

1907   Wilbur goes to France; Alexander Graham Bell and others form the Aerial Experiment Association.

1908   Wilbur flies at Le Mans and Pau, France; Orville is injured and Lieutenant Selfridge is killed at Fort Myer, Virginia.

1909   Hudson-Fulton Exhibition in New York City; Wilbur flies around Statue of Liberty and later flies around Manhattan Island.

1910   The Wrights break with Octave Chanute; legal battles begin between the Wrights and Glenn Curtiss.

1912   Wilbur Wright dies in Dayton.

1914   The Wright family moves into Hawthorn Hill mansion.

1917   Bishop Milton Wright dies.

1926   Katharine Wright marries.

1927	Charles Lindbergh flies from New York to Paris.
1929	Katharine Wright dies.
1948	Orville Wright dies.
1956	Charlie Taylor dies.

NOTES

CHAPTER 1

1. Tom D. Crouch, *First Flight: The Wright Brothers and the Invention of the Airplane* (Washington, D.C.: National Park Service, 2003), 75.
2. Ibid.
3. Amos I. Root, "Our Homes," *Gleanings in Bee Culture*, January 1, 1905, 36.
4. Ibid.
5. Ibid., 38.
6. Ibid.

CHAPTER 2

7. Crouch, *First Flight*, 20.
8. Vernon, "The Flying Man: Otto Lilienthal's Flying Machine," *McClure's*, August 1894, 324.
9. Ibid., 327.
10. Marvin W. McFarland, ed., *The Papers of Wilbur and Orville Wright*, vol. 1 (New York: McGraw Hill, 1953), 4.

CHAPTER 3

11. McFarland, *The Papers of Wilbur and Orville Wright,* vol. 1, 4.
12. Ibid., 15.
13. Ibid., 18.
14. Ibid., 21.

CHAPTER 4

15. McFarland, *The Papers of Wilbur and Orville Wright,* vol. 1, 29.
16. Ibid., 39.
17. Ibid., 34.

18. Ibid., 44.
19. Ibid., 41.
20. Ibid., 101
21. Ibid., 100.
22. Ibid.

CHAPTER 5

23. McFarland, *The Papers of Wilbur and Orville Wright,* vol. 1, 127.
24. Ibid., 148.
25. Ibid., 272.
26. Ibid., 283.

CHAPTER 6

27. Crouch, *First Flight*, 54.
28. Alice Collins Goodyear, ed., *Flight: A Celebration of 100 Years in Art and Literature* (New York: Welcome Books, 2003), 20.
29. John Evangelist Walsh, *One Day at Kitty Hawk: The Untold Story of the Wright Brothers* (New York: Thomas Y. Crowell, 1975), 131.
30. McFarland, *The Papers of Wilbur and Orville Wright,* vol. 1, 391.
31. Ibid., 394.
32. Ibid., 395.
33. Ibid., 396.
34. Goodyear, *Flight: A Celebration of 100 Years in Art and Literature*, 33.
35. Walsh, *One Day at Kitty Hawk: The Untold Story of the Wright Brothers*, 148.

CHAPTER 7

36. Guy Murchie, *Song of the Sky* (Boston: Houghton Mifflin Company, 1954), 118.
37. McFarland, ed., *The Papers of Wilbur and Orville Wright,* vol. 1, 442
38. Ibid., 468.
39. James Tobin, *To Conquer the Air: The Wright Brothers and the Great Race for Flight* (New York: The Free Press, 2003), 226.
40. McFarland, ed., *The Papers of Wilbur and Orville Wright,* vol. 1, 517–518.

CHAPTER 8

41. McFarland, ed., *The Papers of Wilbur and Orville Wright,* vol. 2, 793.
42. Ibid., 800.
43. Ibid., 886–887.
44. Ibid., 912.
45. Noah Adams, *The Flyers: In Search of Wilbur and Orville Wright* (New York: Crown Publishers, 2003), 103.
46. Ibid., 106.

CHAPTER 9

47. *New York Times,* September 24, 1909.
48. Ibid.
49. Ibid.
50. Ibid.
51. *New York Times,* September 30, 1909.

CHAPTER 10

52. McFarland, ed., *The Papers of Wilbur and Orville Wright,* vol. 2.
53. Ibid., 983.
54. Ibid., 986.
55. Quoted in *New York Times,* May 31, 1912.
56. McFarland, ed., *The Papers of Wilbur and Orville Wright,* vol. 2, 1,046.

BIBLIOGRAPHY

Adams, Noah. *The Flyers: In Search of Wilbur and Orville Wright.* New York: Crown Publishers, 2003.

Crouch, Tom D. *First Flight: The Wright Brothers and the Invention of the Airplane.* Washington, D.C.: National Park Service, 2003.

Evans, Harold, Gail Buckland, and David Lefer. *They Made America: From the Steam Engine to the Search Engine: Two Centuries of Innovators.* New York: Little, Brown & Co., 2004.

Goodyear, Alice Collins, ed. *Flight: A Celebration of 100 Years in Art and Literature.* New York: Welcome Books, 2003.

Kelly, Fred C. *The Wright Brothers: A Biography Authorized by Orville Wright.* New York: Harcourt Brace & Company, 1943.

Murchie, Guy. *Song of the Sky.* Boston: Houghton Mifflin Company, 1954.

Root, Amos I. "Our Homes." *Gleanings in Bee Culture,* January 1, 1905.

Taylor, Charles E. "My Story of the Wright Brothers," as told to Robert S. Ball. *Collier's Magazine,* December 25, 1948.

Tobin, James. *To Conquer the Air: The Wright Brothers and the Great Race for Flight.* New York: The Free Press, 2003.

Walsh, John Evangelist. *One Day at Kitty Hawk: The Untold Story of the Wright Brothers.* New York: Thomas Y. Crowell, 1975.

Williams, Trevor I. *A History of Invention: From Stone Axes to Silicon Chips.* New York: Facts on File, 1987.

Wright, Orville. *How We Invented the Airplane: An Illustrated History.* Mineola, N.Y.: Dover Publications, 1988.

Further Reading

Crouch, Tom D. *First Flight: The Wright Brothers and the Invention of the Airplane.* Washington, D.C.: National Park Service, 2003.

Evans, Harold, Gail Buckland, and David Lefer. *They Made America: From the Steam Engine to the Search Engine: Two Centuries of Innovators.* New York: Little, Brown & Co., 2004.

Goodyear, Alice Collins, ed. *Flight: A Celebration of 100 Years in Art and Literature.* New York: Welcome Books, 2003.

Tobin, James. *To Conquer the Air: The Wright Brothers and the Great Race for Flight.* New York: The Free Press, 2003.

Walsh, John Evangelist. *One Day at Kitty Hawk: The Untold Story of the Wright Brothers.* New York: Thomas Y. Crowell, 1975.

Williams, Trevor I. *A History of Invention: From Stone Axes to Silicon Chips.* New York: Facts on File, 1987.

WEB SITES

Wright Brothers History: U.S. Centennial of Flight Commission
http://www.centennialofflight.gov/wbh/index.htm

The Henry Ford Museum: The Wright Brothers
http://www.hfmgv.org/exhibits/wright/

National Air and Space Museum: The Wright Brothers: The Invention of the Aerial Age
http://www.nasm.si.edu/wrightbrothers/

The Wright Brothers National Memorial
http://www.nps.gov/wrbr/

Writings of Wilbur and Orville Wright

http://www.wam.umd.edu/~stwright/WrBr/Wright_articles.html

Reliving the Wright Way

http://wright.nasa.gov/

PICTURE CREDITS

INDEX

About the Author

SAMUEL WILLARD CROMPTON never flew as an airplane passenger until he was 23, but the fascination that began then remains today. A professor of history, he teaches in his native western Massachusetts. Crompton is the author or editor of more than 40 books, primarily on history and notable historical figures. He is also a major contributor to the 24-volume *American National Biography*.